TH

ENDI

THE DOCTRINE OF ENDLESS PUNISHMENT

W.G.T. Shedd

THE BANNER OF TRUTH TRUST

THE BANNER OF TRUTH TRUST
3 Murrayfield Road, Edinburgh EH12 6EL
PO Box 621, Carlisle, Pennsylvania 17013, USA

*

First published 1885
First Banner of Truth edition 1986
Reprinted 1990
Reprinted 1998

ISBN 0 85151 754 4

*

Printed in Finland by
WSOY

CONTENTS.

PREFACE.

At the request of the editor of the North American Review, the author of this book prepared an argument in defence of the doctrine of Endless Punishment, which was published in the number of that periodical for February, 1885. It was agreed that the writer should have the right to republish it at a future time. Only the rational argument was presented in the article. The author now reproduces it, adding the Biblical argument, and a brief historical sketch.

Every doctrine has its day to be attacked, and defended. Just now, that of Eternal Retribution is strenuously combated, not only outside of the church, but to some extent within it. Whoever preaches it is said, by some, not "to preach to the times"—as if the sin of this time were privileged, and stood in a different relation to the law and judgment of God, from that of other times.

The argument from Scripture here given turns principally upon the meaning of Sheol and Hades, and of the adjective *αἰώνιος*. In determining the signification of the former, the author has relied mainly upon the logic and aim of the inspired writers. The reasoning of a writer is a clue to his technical terms. When his object unquestionably is to alarm and deter, it is rational to infer that his phraseology has a meaning in his own mind that is adapted to this. When, therefore, the wicked are threatened with a Sheol and a Hades, it must be an erroneous interpretation that empties them of all the force of a threat. And such is the interpretation which denies that either term denotes the place of retributive suffering.

It is freely acknowledged, that if the meaning of Sheol, or Hades, is to be derived from the usage of a majority of the fathers, and the schoolmen generally, it has no special and exclusive reference to the wicked, and is not of the nature of an evil for them alone. If Sheol, or Hades, is nothing but an underworld for all souls, then it is morally nondescriptive, and whatever of danger there may be in an underworld pertains alike to the righteous and the wicked. But if the Scriptures themselves, and their interpretation by a portion of the fathers, and the reformers generally, are consulted, it is claimed that the position taken in this book, that Sheol, or Hades, is the equivalent of the modern Hell, will hold. It is with eschatology as it is with ecclesiastical polity. If the authority of the Post Nicene fathers and the schoolmen is conceded to be the chief determinant of the questions at issue, the prelatist will carry the day. But if the Bible and the interpretation of the Apostolic and Reformation churches are appealed to, he will lose it. The simplicity of the faith was departed from, when under Hellenizing influences in the church the Heathen Orcus was substituted for the Biblical Hades. A superstitious and materializing eschatology came in along with the corruption of the Christian system, and held sway for a thousand years, until the return to the Scriptures themselves by the leaders of the Reformation, restored the older and purer type of doctrine.

Although the author, in the prosecution of the argument, does not turn aside to enlarge upon the awfulness of the doctrine of Endless Punishment, it must not be supposed that he is unimpressed by it. It is a doctrine which throws in its solemn shadows upon even the most careless human life. No man is utterly indifferent to the possible issues of the great Hereafter. The fall and eternal ruin of an immortal spirit is the most dreadful event conceivable. That some of God's rational and self-determined creatures will forever be in deadly enmity to him, cannot be thought of without sorrow and awe. But from the nature of finite free will, it is a possibility; and it is revealed to us as a fact, as clearly as the facts of incarnation and redemption. Neither the Christian ministry, nor the Christian church, are responsible for the doctrine of Eternal Perdition. It is given in charge to the ministry, and to the church, by the Lord Christ himself, in his last commission, as a truth to be preached to every creature. If they are false to this trust, his message to the church of Ephesus is for them: "Remember from whence thou art fallen, and repent, and do the first works; or else I will come unto thee quickly, and will remove thy candlestick out of his place, except thou repent" (Rev. 2:5). The question, How many are to be saved? the Son of God refused to answer—thereby implying that his mercy is unobligated and sovereign. "I will have mercy on whom I will have mercy" (Rom. 9:15). It becomes man the sinner, not to murmur at this. That incarnate God who has vicariously *suffered* more for man's sin, than any man has or will personally, surely has the right to determine the method and extent of his own self-immolating compassion. To the transgressor who says, "Lord, if thou wilt, thou canst make me clean," he answers, "I will, be thou clean" (Mark 1:40). But to the transgressor who looks upon redemption as something to which he is entitled, he replies, as in the parable, "Is it not lawful for me, to do what I will with mine own?" (Matt. 20:15).

The kindest way, therefore, for both the preacher and the

hearer is, to follow the revealed word of God, and teach the plain and exact truth. Eternal perdition is like any other danger. In order to escape danger, one must believe in it. Disbelief of it is sure destruction. To be forewarned, is to be forearmed. They who foresee an evil, prepare for it and avoid it; but "the simple pass on and are punished." Speaking generally, those who believe that there is a hell, and intelligently fear it, as they are commanded to do by Christ himself, will escape it; and those who deny that there is a hell, and ridicule it, will fall into it. Hence the minister of Christ must be as plain as Christ, as solemn as Christ, and as tender as Christ, in the announcement of this fearful truth. "When he was come near, he beheld the city and wept over it, saying, If thou hadst known, even thou, at least in this thy day, the things which belong unto thy peace! but now they are hid from thine eyes" (Luke 19:41, 42).

The dogmatic bearings of Universalism are not to be overlooked. The rejection of the doctrine of Endless Punishment cuts the ground from under the gospel. Salvation supposes a prior damnation. He who denies that he deserves eternal death cannot be saved from it so long as he persists in his denial. If his denial is the truth, he needs no salvation. If his denial is an error, the error prevents penitence for sin, and this prevents pardon. No error, consequently, is more fatal than that of Universalism. It blots out the attribute of retributive justice; transmutes sin into misfortune, instead of guilt; turns all suffering into chastisement; converts the piacular work of Christ into moral influence; and makes it a debt due to man, instead of an unmerited boon from God. No tenet is more radical and revolutionizing, in its influence upon the Christian system. The attempt to retain the evangelical theology in connection with it is futile.

The destructive nature of the error is still more apparent in practical theology. Could it be proved that the Christian church have been deceived in finding the doctrine of Endless Punishment in the Christian Scriptures, and that there is no such thing, havoc would be made of all the liturgies of the Church, as well as of its literature. Consider the following petition from the "Morning Prayer for Families," in the book of Common Prayer used in the Episcopal church: "Keep in our minds a lively remembrance of that great day in which we must give a strict account of our thoughts, words, and actions, and according to the works done in the body be eternally rewarded or punished by him whom thou hast appointed the Judge of quick and dead, thy Son Jesus Christ our Lord." Suppose, after uttering this petition, the person to say to himself: "There is no eternal punishment." Consider, again, that searching and anguished cry from the Litany: "From thy wrath, and from everlasting damnation, Good Lord, deliver us," and imagine a bystander to say to the soul that has just agonized this prayer: "Thou fool, there is no everlasting damnation." And the effect of this denial is equally destructive in devotional literature. Take the doctrine of eternal perdition, and the antithetic doctrine of eternal salvation, out of the Confessions of Augustine; out of the Sermons of Chrysostom; out of the Imitation of à Kempis; out of Bunyan's Pilgrim's Progress; out of Jeremy Taylor's Holy Living and Dying; out of Baxter's Saints' Everlasting Rest; and what is left?

UNION THEOLOGICAL SEMINARY,
NEW YORK, November 18, 1885.

PREFACE TO THE SECOND EDITION.

THE author avails himself of the opportunity afforded by the issue of a second edition of this volume, to revise and somewhat enlarge it. He has added pp. 163–169 to the body of the work, for the purpose of calling attention to the important truth that the necessity for endless retribution is grounded in the action of *man*, not of God. "God," says Augustine (Trinity IV. xii.), "made not death (Wisdom 1:13), since He was not Himself the cause of death; but yet death was inflicted on the sinner through His most just retribution. Just as the judge inflicts punishment on the guilty; yet it is not the justice of the judge, but the *desert of the crime*, which is the cause of the punishment" It is the author of sin who is the author of hell. The opponent of endless punishment should, therefore, level his reproaches against sin and the sinner, not against holiness and God.

An Appendix has also been added to the volume, for the purpose of expanding and strengthening some of the positions taken in it. The material is to a considerable extent derived from the writings of others. It is put into the form of notes, which are referred to by their several numbers on the pages of the volume.

NEW YORK, November 4, 1887.

ENDLESS PUNISHMENT.

CHAPTER I.

THE HISTORY OF THE DOCTRINE.

The common opinion in the Ancient church was, that the future punishment of the impenitent wicked is endless. This was the catholic faith; as much so as belief in the trinity. But as there were some church fathers who deviated from the creed of the church respecting the doctrine of the trinity, so there were some who dissented from it in respect to that of eternal retribution. The deviation in eschatology, however, was far less extensive than in trinitarianism. The Semi-Arian and Arian heresies involved and troubled the Ancient church much more seriously, than did the Universalism of that period. Long controversies, ending in œcumenical councils and formulated statements, were the consequence of the trinitarian errors, but no œcumenical council, and no authoritative counter-statement, was required to prevent the spread of the tenet of Restoration. Having so little even seeming support in scripture and reason, it gradually died out of the Ancient church by its own intrinsic mortality. Neander (II., 737), speaking of the second period in his arrangement (312–590), when there was more Restorationism than in the first, says: "The doctrine of eternal punishment continued, as in the preceding period, to be dominant in the creed of the church. Yet, in the Oriental church, in which, with the exception of those subjects immediately connected with the doctrinal controversies, there was greater freedom and latitude of development, many respectable church teachers still stood forth, without injuring their reputation for orthodoxy, as advocates of the opposite doctrine, until the time when the Origenistic disputes caused the agreement with Origen in respect to this point also [viz., Restorationism] to be considered as something decidedly heretical." Hagenbach (History of Doctrine, § 78) says of the period down to A.D. 250: "Notions more or less gross prevailed concerning the punishment of the wicked, which most of the fathers regarded as eternal."

The principal deviation from the catholic doctrine of endless retribution was in the Alexandrine school, founded by Clement and Origen. The position taken by them was, that "the punishments of the condemned are not eternal, but only remedial; the devil himself being capable of amelioration" (Gieseler. I. 214). Thus early was the question raised, whether the suffering to which Christ sentences the wicked is for the purpose of correcting and educating the transgressor, or of vindicating and satisfying the law he has broken—a question which is the key to the whole controversy. For, if the individual criminal is of greater consequence than the universal law, then the suffering must refer principally to him and his interests. But if the law is of more importance than any individual, then the suffering must refer principally to it.[1]

Origen's Restorationism grew naturally out of his view of human liberty. He held that the liberty of indifference and the power of contrary choice, instead of simple self-determination, are the substance of freedom. These belong inalienably and forever to the nature of the finite will. They cannot be destroyed, even by apostasy and sin. Consequently, there is forever a possibility of a self-conversion of the will in either direction. Free will may fall into sin at any time; and free will may turn to God at any time. This led to Origen's theory of an endless alternation of falls and recoveries, of hells and heavens; so that practically he taught nothing but a hell. For, as Augustine (City of God, XXI., 17) remarks, in his refutation of Origen, "heaven with the prospect of losing it is misery." "Origen's theory," says Neander (I., 656), "concerning the necessary mutability of will in created beings, led him to infer that evil, ever germinating afresh, would still continue to render necessary new processes of purification, and new worlds destined for the restoration of fallen beings, until all should again be brought back from manifoldness to unity, so that there was to be a constant interchange between fall and redemption, between unity and manifoldness."

Traces, more or less distinct, of a belief in the future restoration of the wicked are found in Didymus of Alexandria, the two Gregories, and also in Diodore of Tarsus, and Theodore of Mopsuestia—the leaders of the Antiochian school. All of these were more or less under the influence of Origen. Origen's opinions, however, both in trinitarianism and eschatology, were strongly combated in his own time by the great body of contemporary fathers, and subsequently by the church under the lead of Epiphanius, Jerome, and Augustine.

The Mediæval church was virtually a unit in holding the doctrine of Endless Punishment. The Reformation churches, both Lutheran and Calvinistic, adopted the historical and catholic opinion.

Since the Reformation, Universalism, Restorationism, and Annihilation, have been asserted by some sects and many individuals. But these tenets have never been adopted by those ecclesiastical denominations which hold, in their integrity, the cardinal doctrines of the trinity and incarnation, the apostasy and redemption, although they have exerted some influence within these denominations. None of the evangelical churches have introduced the doctrine of Universalism, in any form of it, into their symbolical books. The denial of endless punishment is usually associated with the denial of those tenets which are logically and closely connected with it—such as original sin, vicarious atonement, and regeneration. Of these, vicarious atonement is the most incompatible of any with universal salvation; because the latter doctrine, as has been observed, implies that suffering for sin is remedial only, while the former implies that it is retributive. Suffering that is merely educational does not require a vicarious atonement in order to release from it. But suffering that is judicial and punitive can be released from the transgressor, only by being inflicted upon a substitute. He, therefore, who denies personal penalty must, logically, deny vicarious penalty. If the sinner himself is not obliged by justice to suffer in order to satisfy the law he has violated, then, certainly, no one needs suffer for him for this purpose.

Within the present century, Universalism has obtained a stronger hold upon German theology than upon any other, and has considerably vitiated it. It grew up in connection with the rationalism and pantheism which have been more powerful in Germany than elsewhere. Rationalism has many of the characteristics of deism, and is vehemently polemic toward evangelical truth. That it should combat the doctrines of sin and atonement is natural. Pantheism, on the other hand, has to some extent been mingled with evangelical elements. A class of anti-rationalistic theologians, in Germany, whose opinions are influenced more or less by Spinoza and Schelling, accept the doctrines of the trinity, incarnation, apostasy, and redemption, and assert the ultimate recovery from sin of all mankind. Schleiermacher, the founder of this school, whose system is a remarkable blending of the gospel and pantheism, has done much toward the spread of Restorationism. The following are the objections which this theologian (Glaubenslehre, § 163, Anhang) makes to eternal damnation: "1. Christ's words in Matt. 25: 46; Mark 9: 44; John 5: 29, are figurative. 2. The passage 1 Cor. 15: 25, 26, teaches that all evil shall be overcome. 3. Misery cannot increase, but must decrease. If it is bodily misery, custom habituates to endurance, and there is less and less suffering instead of more and more.[2] If, on the other hand, it is mental suffering, this is remorse. The damned suffer more remorse in hell than they do upon earth. This proves that they are better men in hell than upon earth. They cannot, therefore, grow more wretched in hell, but grow less so as they grow more remorseful. 4. The sympathy which the saved have with their former companions, who are in hell, will prevent the happiness of the saved. The world of mankind, and also the whole universe, is so connected that the endless misery of a part will destroy the happiness of the remainder.[3] These objections appeal mainly to reason. But the two assumptions, that hell is abolished by becoming used to it, and that remorse is of the nature of virtue, do not commend themselves to the intuitive convictions.

Besides the disciples of Schleiermacher, there are trinitarian theologians standing upon the position of theism, who adopt some form of Universalism. Nitzsch (Dogmatics, § 219) teaches Restorationism. He cites in support of it only two passages out of the entire scriptures—namely, 1 Pet., 3: 19, which speaks of the "preaching to the spirits in prison;" and Heb. 11: 39, 40: "These received not the promises." These two passages Nitzsch explains, as teaching that "there are traces of a capacity in another state of existence for comprehending salvation, and for a change and purification of mind;" and upon them solely he founds the sweeping assertion, that "it is the apostolical view, that for those who were unable in this world to know Christ in his truth and grace, there is a knowledge of the Redeemer in the other state of existence which is never inoperative, but is either judicial or quickening."

Rothe (Dogmatics, Th. II., Abth., ii. §§ 46–49, 124–131) contends for the annihilation of the impenitent wicked, in the sense of the extinction of self-consciousness. Yet he asserts that the aim of penalty is requital, and the satisfaction of justice—an aim that would be defeated by the extinction of remorse. Julius Müller (Sin, II., 191, 418, 425) affirms that the sin against the Holy Ghost is never forgiven, because it implies such a hardness in sin as is incapable of penitence. But he holds that the offer of forgiveness through Christ will be made to every human being, here or hereafter. "Those who have never in this life had an opportunity of knowing the way of salvation will certainly be placed in a position to accept and enter upon this way of return, if they will, after their life on earth is ended. We may venture to hope that in the interval between death and the judgment many serious misconceptions, which have hindered men from appropriating truth in this life, will be removed." The use of the term "misconception" would seem to imply that some who had the offer of salvation in this life, but had rejected it, will have the opportunity in the next life to correct their error in this. Dorner (Christian Doctrine,

IV., 416–428), after giving the arguments for and against endless punishment, concludes with the remark, that "we must be content with saying that the ultimate fate of individuals, namely, whether all will attain the blessed goal or not, remains veiled in mystery." His further remark, that "there may be those eternally damned, so far as the abuse of freedom continues eternally, but, in this case, man has passed into *another class* of beings," looks in the direction of annihilation—suggesting that sin will finally destroy the humanity of man, and leave him a mere brute. Respecting the future offer of mercy, Dorner asserts that "the final judgment can take place for none before the gospel has been so addressed to him that free appropriation of the same was possible" (Christian Doctrine, III., 77).

Universalism has a slender exegetical basis. The Biblical data are found to be unmanageable, and resort is had to human feeling and sympathy. Its advocates quote sparingly from scripture. In particular, the words of Christ relating to eschatology are left with little citation or interpretation. Actual attempts by the Restorationist, to explain what the words, "Depart from me, ye cursed, into everlasting fire, prepared for the devil and his angels," *really mean*, are rare. The most common device is to dismiss them, as Schleiermacher does, with the remark that they are figurative. Some words of St. Paul, on the other hand, whose views upon sin, election, and predestination, however, are not especially attractive to this class, are made to do yeoman's service. Texts like Rom. 5 : 18, "As judgment came upon all men unto condemnation, so the free gift came upon all men unto justification;" and 1 Cor. 15: 22, "As in Adam all die, so in Christ shall all be made alive;" are explained wholly apart from their context, and by vocalizing the word "all." When St. Paul asserts that "the free gift came upon all men unto justification," this is severed from the preceding verse, in which the "all" are described as "those which receive abundance of grace, and of the gift of righteousness." And when the same apostle affirms that "in Christ shall all be made alive," no notice is taken of the fact mentioned in the succeeding verse, that not all men are "in Christ"—the clause, "they that are Christ's, at his coming," implying that there are some who are *not* "Christ's at his coming."

The paucity of the texts of scripture that can with any plausibility be made to teach Universalism sometimes leads to an ingenuity that is unfavorable to candid exegesis. The endeavor to escape the force of plain revelation introduces unnatural explanations. A curious example of caprice in interpretation is found in Ruetschi's Kritik vom Sündenfall (p. 231). To prove his assertion, that sin by its very nature finally ceases to be, he quotes Rom. 6: 23, "The wages of sin is death." This means, according to him, that sin ultimately consumes and abolishes itself (muss sich schliesslich selbst verzehren und aufheben), and this is its "wages" or punishment. This Essay actually obtained the prize offered by the Hague Association for the defence of the Christian Religion. This specimen of Biblical interpretation is matched by that of a recent advocate of "Conditional Immortality," who contends that Satan taught the natural immortality of the human soul when he said to Eve: "Ye shall not surely die;" and that God taught its natural mortality in the words: "Thou shalt surely die."

CHAPTER II.

THE BIBLICAL ARGUMENT.

The strongest support of the doctrine of Endless Punishment is the teaching of Christ, the Redeemer of man. Though the doctrine is plainly taught in the Pauline Epistles, and other parts of Scripture, yet without the explicit and reiterated statements of God incarnate, it is doubtful whether so awful a truth would have had such a conspicuous place as it always has had in the creed of Christendom. If, in spite of that large mass of positive and solemn threatening of everlasting punishment from the lips of Jesus Christ, which is recorded in the four Gospels, the attempt has nevertheless been made to prove that the tenet is not an integral part of the Christian system, we may be certain that had this portion of Revelation been wanting, this attempt would have been much more frequent, and much more successful. The Apostles enter far less into detailed description, and are far less emphatic upon this solemn theme, than their divine Lord and Master. And well they might be. For as none but God has the right, and would dare, to sentence a soul to eternal misery, for sin; and as none but God has the right, and would dare, to execute the sentence; so none but God has the right, and should presume, to delineate the nature and consequences of this sentence. This is the reason why most of the awful imagery in which the sufferings of the lost are described is found in the discourses of our Lord and Saviour. He took it upon himself to sound the note of warning. He, the Judge of quick and dead, assumed the responsibility of teaching the doctrine of Endless Retribution. "I will forewarn you whom ye shall fear: Fear him who after he hath killed hath power to cast into hell; yea, I say unto you, Fear him." "Nothing," says Dr. Arnold, "is more striking to me, than our Lord's own description of the judgment. It is so inexpressibly forcible, coming from his very own lips, as descriptive of what he himself would do" (Stanley's Life of Arnold, I. 176).

Christ could not have warned men so frequently and earnestly as he did against "the fire that never shall be quenched," and "the worm that dieth not," had he known that there is no future peril fully corresponding to them. That omniscient Being who made the statements respecting the day of judgment, and the final sentence, that are recorded in Matthew 25 : 31–46, could neither have believed nor expected that all men without exception will eventually be holy and happy. To threaten with "everlasting punishment" a class of persons described as "goats upon the left hand" of the Eternal Judge, while knowing at the same time that this class would ultimately have the same holiness and happiness with those described as "sheep upon the right hand" of the judge, would have been both falsehood and folly. The threatening would have been false. For even a long punishment in the future world would not have justified Christ in teaching that this class of mankind are to experience the same retribution with "the devil and his angels;" for these were understood by the Jews, to whom he spoke, to be hopelessly and eternally lost spirits.* And the threatening would have been foolish, because it would have been a *brutum fulmen*, an exaggerated danger, certainly in the mind of its author. And for the persons threatened, it would have been a terror only because they took a different view of it from what its author did—they believing it to be true, and he knowing it to be false!

*Edersheim (Life of Jesus, II. 789) asserts that the schools of Shammai and Hillel both taught the doctrine of eternal punishment. "These schools represented the theological teaching in the time of Christ and his Apostles, showing that the doctrine of Eternal Punishment was held in the days of our Lord, however it may have been afterwards modified." Edersheim adds, that "the doctrine of the eternity of punishment seems to have been held by the Synagogue throughout the whole first century. In the second century, there is a decided difference in Rabbinic opinion; some denying the doctrine of endless retribution. In the third century, there is a reaction and a return to former views."

The mere perusal of Christ's words when he was upon earth, without note or comment upon them, will convince the unprejudiced that the Redeemer of sinners knew and believed, that for impenitent men and devils there is an endless punishment. We solicit a careful reading and pondering of the following well-known passages: "When the Son of man shall come in his glory, and all the holy angels with him, then shall he sit upon the throne of his glory; and before him shall be gathered all nations, and he shall separate them one from another, as a shepherd divideth his sheep from the goats. And he shall set the sheep on his right hand, but the goats on the left. Then shall he say unto them on the left hand, Depart from me, ye cursed, into everlasting fire, prepared for the devil and his angels. And these shall go away into everlasting punishment" (Matt. 25: 31–33, 41, 46). "If thy right hand offend thee, cut it off: it is better for thee to enter into life maimed than having two hands to go into hell, into the fire that never shall be quenched; where their worm dieth not, and the fire is not quenched. And if thy foot offend thee, cut it off: it is better for thee to enter halt into life, than having two feet to be cast into hell, into the fire that never shall be quenched; where their worm dieth not, and the fire is not quenched. And if thine eye offend thee, pluck it out: it is better for thee to enter into the kingdom of God with one eye, than having two eyes to be cast into hell fire: where their worm dieth not, and the fire is not quenched" (Mark 9 : 43–48). "What shall it profit a man, if he shall gain the whole world, and lose his own soul? What is a man advantaged, if he gain the whole world, and be cast away?" (Mark 8 : 36; Luke 9 : 25). "The rich man died and was buried, and in hell he lifted up his eyes being in torments" (Luke 16 : 22, 23). "Fear not them which kill the body, but are not able to kill the soul: but rather fear him which is able to destroy both soul and body in hell" (Matt. 10 : 28). "The Son of man shall send forth his angels, and they shall gather out of his kingdom all things that offend, and them which do iniquity, and shall cast them into a furnace of fire: there shall be wailing and gnashing of teeth" (Matt. 13 : 41, 42). "Many will say to me in that day, Lord, Lord, have we not prophesied in thy name? Then will I profess unto them, I never knew you: depart from me, ye that work iniquity" (Matt. 7 : 22, 23). "He that denieth me before men shall be denied before the angels of God. Unto him that blasphemeth against the Holy Ghost, it shall never be forgiven" (Luke 12 : 9, 10). "Woe unto you, ye blind guides. Ye serpents, ye generation of vipers, how can ye escape the damnation of hell?" (Matt. 23 : 16, 33). "Woe unto that man by whom the Son of man is betrayed! it had been good for that man if he had not been born" (Matt. 26 : 24). "The Lord of that servant will come in a day when he looketh not for him, and at an hour when he is not aware, and will cut him in sunder, and appoint him his portion with unbelievers" (Luke 12 : 46). "He that believeth not shall be damned" (Mark 16 : 16). "Thou Capernaum, which art exalted unto heaven, shalt be brought down to hell" (Matt. 11 : 23). "At the end of the world, the angels shall come forth and sever the wicked from among the just, and shall cast them into the furnace of fire" (Matt. 13 : 49, 50). "Then said Jesus again to them, I go my way, and ye shall seek me, and shall die in your sins: whither I go ye cannot come" (John 8 : 21). "The hour is coming in which all that are in their graves shall hear my voice, and shall come forth; they that have done good, unto the resurrection of life; and they that have done evil, unto the resurrection of damnation" (John 5 : 28, 29).

To all this, add the description of the manner in which Christ will discharge the office of the Eternal Judge. John the Baptist represents him as one "whose fan is in his hand, and he will throughly purge his floor, and gather his wheat into the garner, but will burn up the chaff with unquenchable fire" (Matt. 3 : 12). And Christ describes himself as a householder who will say to the reapers, "Gather ye together first the tares, and bind them in bundles to burn them" (Matt. 13 : 30); as a fisherman "casting a net into the sea, and gathering of every kind; which when it was full he drew to the shore, and sat down and gathered the good into vessels, but cast the bad away" (Matt. 13 : 47, 48); as the bridegroom who took the wise virgins "with him to the marriage," and shut the door upon the foolish (Matt. 25 : 10); and as the man travelling into a far country who delivered talents to his servants, and afterwards reckons with them, rewarding the "good and faithful," and "casting the unprofitable servant into outer darkness, where there shall be weeping and gnashing of teeth" (Matt. 25 : 19–30).

Let the reader now ask himself the question: Do these representations, and this phraseology, make the impression that the future punishment of sin is to be *remedial* and *temporary?* Are they adapted to make this impression? Were they intended to make this impression? Is it possible to believe that that Holy and Divine Person who uttered these fearful and unqualified warnings, eighteen hundred years ago, respecting the destiny of wicked men and devils, knew that a time is coming when there will be no wicked men and devils in the universe of God, and no place of retributive torment? Did Jesus of Nazareth hold an esoteric doctrine of hell—a different view of the final state of the wicked, from that which the common and natural understanding of his language would convey to his hearers, and has conveyed to the great majority of his readers in all time? Did he know that in the far-off future, a day will come when those tremendous scenes which he described—the gathering of all mankind, the separation of the evil from the good, the curse pronounced upon the former and the blessing upon the latter—will be looked back upon by all mankind as "an unsubstantial pageant faded," as a dream that is passed, and a watch in the night?

Having thus noticed the positive and explicit nature of Christ's teaching, we now proceed to examine the terms employed in Scripture to denote the abode of the lost, and the nature of their punishment.

The Old Testament term for the future abode of the wicked, and the place of future punishment, is Sheol (שְׁאוֹל). This word, which is translated by Hades (ᾅδης) in the Septuagint, has two significations: 1. The place of future retribution. 2. The grave.

Before presenting the proof of this position, we call attention to the fact, that it agrees with the explanation of Sheol and Hades common in the Early Patristic and Reformation churches, and disagrees with that of the Later Patristic, the Mediæval, and a part of the Modern Protestant church. It agrees also with the interpretation generally given to these words in the versions of the Scriptures made since the Reformation, in the various languages of the world.

The view of the Reformers is stated in the following extract from the Schaff-Herzog encyclopædia (Article Hades): "The Protestant churches rejected, with purgatory and its abuses, the whole idea of a middle state, and taught simply two states and places—heaven for believers, and hell for unbelievers. Hades was identified with Gehenna, and hence both terms were translated alike in the Protestant versions. The English (as also Luther's German) version of the New Testament translates Hades and Gehenna by the same word 'hell,' and thus obliterates the important distinction between the realm of the dead (or nether-world, spirit-world), and the place of torment or eternal punishment; but in the Revision of 1881 the distinction is restored, and the term Hades introduced." The same change is made in the Revised Old Testament, published in 1885. The Authorized version renders Sheol sometimes by "hell," in the sense of the place of punishment, and sometimes by "grave"—the context determining which is the meaning. The Revisers substitute "Sheol" for "hell," and whenever they leave the word "grave" in the text, add the note: "The Hebrew is Sheol," in order, as they say, "to indicate that it is not the place of burial." Had they been content with the mere transliteration of Sheol, the reader might interpret for himself. But in the preface to their version they become commentators, and interpret for him. They deny that Sheol means "hell" in the sense of "the place of torment," and assert that it "signifies the abode of departed spirits, and corresponds to the Greek Hades, or the Underworld" (Preface to the Revised Old Testament).

The meaning of an important technical term, such as Sheol, must be determined, certainly in part, by the connection of thought, and the general tenor of Scripture. An interpretation must not be put upon it that will destroy the symmetry of doctrine. Whether Sheol is from שָׁאַל or שָׁעַל, or any other merely linguistic particular, will not of itself decide the question whether it denotes the Heathen Orcus, or the Christian Hell. That Sheol is a fearful punitive evil, mentioned by the sacred writers to deter men from sin, lies upon the face of the Old Testament, and any interpretation that essentially modifies this must therefore be erroneous. But such an essential modification is made by denying that it is the place of torment, and converting it into a promiscuous and indiscriminate abode for all disembodied spirits. The indiscriminateness nullifies the evil, and the fear of it. A successful version of the Bible requires the union of philology and theology. A translation of Scripture made wholly upon assumed philological grounds, and independent of the analogy of faith, would be certain to contain errors. The general system of Christian truth, and the connection of ideas, confessedly controls the explanation of such terms as πίστις, ζωή, πνεῦμα, and λόγος. Merely to apply classical and lexical philology in these cases, would lead to misconception. Even, therefore, if it were conceded that the Greek and Hebrew learning of the English Revisers is superior to that of the age of Usher and Selden, it would not necessarily follow that the truth in this instance is with them, and not with their predecessors. That they may have been under a dogmatic prepossession, and have interpreted Scripture by mythology, and the spurious clause of a creed, instead of by Scripture itself, is a possibility.[4]

I. In the first place, Sheol signifies the place of future retribution.

1. This is proved, first, by the fact that it is denounced against sin and sinners, and not against the righteous. It is a place to which the *wicked* are sent, in distinction from the good. "The wicked in a moment go down to sheol" (Job 21: 13). "The wicked shall be turned into sheol, and all the nations that forget God" (Ps. 9:17). "Her steps take hold on sheol" (Prov. 5:5). "Her guests are in the depths of sheol" (Prov 9:

18). "Thou shalt beat thy child with a rod, and shalt deliver his soul from sheol" (Prov. 23 : 14). "A fire is kindled in my anger, and it shall burn to the lowest sheol" (Deut. 32 : 22). "If I ascend up into heaven, thou art there; if I make my bed in sheol [the contrary of heaven], behold thou art there" (Ps. 139 : 8). "The way of life is above to the wise, that he may depart from sheol beneath" (Prov. 15 : 24). "Sheol is naked before him, and destruction [Abaddon, Rev. ver.] hath no covering" (Job 26 : 6). "Sheol and destruction [Abaddon, Rev. ver.] are before the Lord" (Prov. 15:11). "Sheol and destruction [Abaddon, Rev. ver.] are never full" (Prov. 27: 20). If in these last three passages the Revised rendering be adopted, it is still more evident that Sheol denotes Hell; for Abaddon is the Hebrew for Apollyon, who is said to be "the angel and king of the bottomless pit" (Rev. 9 : 11).[5]

There can be no rational doubt, that in this class of Old Testament texts the wicked are warned of a future *evil* and *danger*. The danger is, that they shall be sent to Sheol. The connection of thought requires, therefore, that Sheol in such passages have the same meaning as the modern Hell, and like this have an *exclusive* reference to the wicked. Otherwise, it is not a warning. To give it a meaning that makes it the common residence of the good and evil, is to destroy its force as a Divine menace. If Sheol be merely a promiscuous underworld for all souls, then to be "turned into sheol" is no more a menace for the sinner than for the saint, and consequently a menace for neither. In order to be of the nature of an alarm for the wicked, Sheol must be something that pertains to them alone. If it is shared with the good, its power to terrify is gone. If the good man goes to Sheol, the wicked man will not be afraid to go with him. It is no answer to this, to say that Sheol contains two divisions, Hades and Paradise, and that the wicked go to the former. This is not in the Biblical text, or in its connection. The wicked who are threatened with Sheol, as the punishment of their wickedness, are not threatened with a part of Sheol, but with the *whole* of it. Sheol is one, undivided, and homogeneous in the inspired representation. The subdivision of it into heterogeneous compartments, is a conception imported into the Bible from the Greek and Roman classics. The Old Testament knows nothing of a Sheol that is partly an evil, and partly a good. The Biblical Sheol is always an evil, and nothing but an evil. When the human body goes down to Sheol in the sense of the "grave," this is an evil. And when the human soul goes down to Sheol in the sense of "hell and retribution," this is an evil. Both are threatened, as the penalty of sin, to the wicked, but never to the righteous.

Consequently, in the class of passages of which we are speaking, "going down to sheol" denotes something more dreadful than "going down to the grave," or than entering the so-called underworld of departed spirits. To say that "the wicked shall be turned into sheol," implies that the righteous shall *not* be; just as to say that "they who obey not the gospel of our Lord Jesus Christ shall be punished with everlasting destruction" (2 Thess. 1 : 8, 9), implies that those who do obey it shall *not* be. To say that the "steps" of the prostitute "take hold on sheol," is the same as to say that "whoremongers shall have their part in the lake which burneth with fire and brimstone" (Rev. 21 : 8). To "deliver the soul of a child from sheol" by parental discipline, is not to deliver him either from the grave, or from a spirit-world, but from the future torment that awaits the morally undisciplined. In mentioning Sheol in such a connection, the inspired writer is not mentioning a region that is common alike to the righteous and the wicked. This would defeat his purpose to warn the latter.* Sheol, when

* "The meaning of the Hebrew word Sheol is doubtful, but I have not hesitated to translate it hell. I do not find fault with those who translate it grave, but it is certain that the prophet means something more than common death; otherwise he would say nothing else concerning the wicked, than what would also happen to all the faithful in common with them" (Calvin on Ps. 9:17).

denounced to the wicked, must be as peculiar to them, and as much confined to them, as when "the lake of fire and brimstone" is denounced to them. All such Old Testament passages teach that those who go to Sheol suffer from the wrath of God, as the Eternal Judge who punishes iniquity. The words: "The wicked is snared in the work of his own hands. The wicked shall be turned into sheol, and all the nations that forget God" (Ps. 9: 16, 17), are as much of the nature of a Divine menace against sin, as the words, "In the day thou eatest thereof, thou shalt surely die" (Gen. 2 : 17). And the interpretation which eliminates the idea of penal suffering from the former, to be consistent, should eliminate it from the latter.

Accordingly, these texts must be read in connection with, and interpreted by, that large class of texts in the Old Testament which represent God as a *judge*, and assert a future *judgment*, and a future *resurrection* for this purpose. "Shall not the judge of all the earth do right?" (Gen. 18:25). "To me belongeth vengeance, and recompense; their feet shall slide in due time" (Deut. 32 : 35). "Enoch the seventh from Adam prophesied of these, saying, Behold the Lord cometh with ten thousand of his saints to execute judgment upon all, and to convince all that are ungodly among them of all their ungodly deeds which they have ungodly committed" (Jude 14, 15).

"The wicked is reserved to the day of destruction. They shall be brought forth to the day of wrath" (Job 21 : 30). "The ungodly shall not stand in the judgment; the way of the ungodly shall perish" (Ps. 1 : 5, 6). "Verily, he is a God that judgeth in the earth" (Ps. 58 : 11). "Who knoweth the power of thine anger? even according to thy fear, so is thy wrath" (Ps. 90 : 11). "O Lord God, to whom vengeance belongeth, shew thyself. Lift up thyself, thou Judge of the earth: render a reward to the proud" (Ps. 94 : 1, 2). "There is a way that seemeth right unto a man, but the end thereof are the ways of death" (Prov. 16 : 25). "God shall judge the righteous and the wicked: for there is a time for every purpose, and every work" (Eccl. 3 : 17). "Walk in the ways of thine heart, and in the sight of thine eyes; but know thou that for all these things God will bring thee into judgment" (Eccl. 11 : 9). "God shall bring every work into judgment, with every secret thing, whether it be good, or whether it be evil" (Eccl. 12 : 14). "The sinners in Zion are afraid; fearfulness hath surprised the hypocrites. Who among us shall dwell with devouring fire? who among us shall dwell with devouring burnings?" (Is. 33 : 14). Of "the men that have transgressed against God," it is said that their "worm shall not die, neither shall their fire be quenched" (Is. 66 : 24). "I beheld till the thrones were cast down, and the

Ancient of days did sit. His throne was like the fiery flame, and his wheels like burning fire; thousand thousands ministered unto him, and ten thousand times ten thousand stood before him: the judgment was set, and the books were opened" (Dan. 7 : 9, 10). "Many of them that sleep in the dust of the earth shall awake, some to everlasting life, and some to shame and everlasting contempt" (Dan. 12 : 2). "The Lord hath sworn by the excellency of Jacob, Surely I never will forget any of their works" (Amos 8 : 7). "They shall be mine, saith the Lord of hosts, in the day when I make up my jewels" (Mal. 3 : 17).[6]

A final judgment, unquestionably, supposes a *place* where the sentence is executed. Consequently, these Old Testament passages respecting the final judgment throw a strong light upon the meaning of Sheol, and make it certain, in the highest degree, that it denotes the world where the penalty resulting from the verdict of the Supreme Judge is to be experienced by the transgressor. The "wicked," when sentenced at the last judgment, are "turned into sheol," as "idolaters and all liars," when sentenced, "have their part in the lake which burneth with fire and brimstone" (Rev. 21 : 8).

2. A second proof that Sheol is the proper name for Hell, in the Old Testament, is the fact that there is no other proper name for it in the whole

volume—for Tophet is metaphorical, and rarely employed. If Sheol is not the place where the wrath of God falls upon the transgressor, there is no place mentioned in the Old Testament where it does. But it is utterly improbable that the final judgment would be announced so clearly as it is under the Old Dispensation, and yet the place of retributive suffering be undesignated. In modern theology, the Judgment and Hell are correlates; each implying the other, each standing or falling with the other. In the Old Testament theology, the Judgment and Sheol sustain the same relations. The proof that Sheol does not signify Hell would, virtually, be the proof that the doctrine of Hell is not contained in the Old Testament; and this would imperil the doctrine of the final judgment. Universalism receives strong support from all versions and commentaries which take the idea of retribution out of the term Sheol. No texts that contain the word can be cited to prove either a future sentence, or a future suffering. They only prove that there is a world of disembodied spirits, whose moral character and condition cannot be inferred from anything in the signification of Sheol; because the good are in Sheol, and the wicked are in Sheol. When it is merely said of a deceased person that he is in the world of spirits, it is impossible to decide whether he is holy or sinful, happy or miserable.

3. A third proof that Sheol, in these passages, denotes the dark abode of the wicked, and the state of future suffering, is found in those Old Testament texts which speak of the contrary bright abode of the righteous, and of their state of blessedness. According to the view we are combating, Paradise is in Sheol, and constitutes a part of it. But there is too great a contrast between the two abodes of the good and evil, to allow of their being brought under one and the same gloomy and terrifying term Sheol. When "the Lord put a word in Balaam's mouth," Balaam said, "Let me die the death of the righteous, and let my last end be like his" (Num. 23 : 5, 10). The Psalmist describes this "last end of the righteous" in the following terms: "My flesh shall rest in hope. Thou wilt show me the path of life; in thy presence is fulness of joy; at thy right hand there are pleasures for evermore" (Ps. 16:11). "As for me, I will behold thy face in righteousness; I shall be satisfied when I awake with thy likeness" (Ps. 17:15). "God will redeem my soul from the power of sheol; for he shall receive me" (Ps. 49:15). "Thou shalt guide me with thy counsel, and afterwards receive me to glory. Whom have I in heaven but thee?" (Ps. 73:24). In like manner, Isaiah (25:8) says, respecting the righteous, that "the Lord God will swallow up death in victory, and will wipe away

tears from all faces;" and Solomon asserts that "the righteous hath hope in his death" (Prov. 14:32). These descriptions of the blessedness of the righteous when they die have nothing in common with the Old Testament conception of Sheol, and cannot possibly be made to agree with it. The "anger" of God "burns to the lowest sheol;" which implies that it burns through the whole of Sheol, from top to bottom. The wicked are "turned" into Sheol, and "in a moment go down" to Sheol; but the good are not "turned" into "glory," nor do they "in a moment go down" to "the right hand of God." The "presence" of God, the "right hand" of God, the "glory" to which the Psalmist is to be received, and the "heaven" which he longs for, are certainly not in the dreadful Sheol. They do not constitute one of its compartments. If, between death and the resurrection, the disembodied spirit of the Psalmist is in "heaven," at the "right hand" of God, in his "presence," and beholding his "glory," it is not in a dismal underworld. There is not a passage in the Old Testament that asserts, or in any way suggests, that the light of the Divine countenance, and the blessedness of communion with God, are enjoyed in Sheol. Sheol, in the Old Testament, is gloom, and only gloom, and gloomy continually. Will any one seriously contend that in the passage: "Enoch walked with God: and he was not; for God took him," it would harmonize with the idea of "walking with God," and with the Old Testament conception of Sheol, to supply the ellipsis by saying that "God took him to sheol?" Was Sheol that "better country, that is, an *heavenly*," which the Old Testament saints "desired," and to attain which they "were tortured, not accepting deliverance?" (Heb. 11:16, 35).

4. A fourth proof that Sheol is the place of future retribution, is its inseparable connection with spiritual and eternal death. The Old Testament, like the New, designates the punishment of the wicked by the term "death." And spiritual death is implied, as well as physical. Such is the meaning in Gen. 2:17. The death there threatened is the very same θάνατος to which St. Paul refers in Rom. 5:12, and which "passed upon all men" by reason of the transgression in Eden. Spiritual death is clearly taught in Deut. 30:15, "I have set before thee this day life and good, and death and evil;" in Jer. 21:8, "I set before you the way of life, and the way of death;" in Ezek. 18:32; 33:11, "I have no pleasure in the death of the wicked; but that the wicked turn from his way and live;" in Prov. 8:36, "All they that hate me love death." Spiritual death is also taught, by implication, in those Old Testament passages which speak of spiritual life as its contrary. "As

righteousness tendeth to life, so he that pursueth evil pursueth it to his own death" (Prov. 11:19). "Whoso findeth me findeth life" (Prov. 8:35). "He is in the way of life that keepeth instruction" (Prov. 10:17). "Thou wilt show me the path of life" (Ps. 16:11). "With thee is the fountain of life" (Ps. 36:9). "There the Lord commanded the blessing, even life for evermore" (Ps. 133:3).

Sheol is as inseparably associated with spiritual death and perdition, in the Old Testament, as Hades is in the New Testament, and as Hell is in the common phraseology of the Christian Church. "Sheol is naked before him, and destruction hath no covering" (Job 26:6). "Sheol and destruction are before the Lord" (Prov. 15:11). "Sheol and destruction are never full" (Prov. 27:20). "Her house is the way to sheol, going down to the chambers of death" (Prov. 7:27). "Her house inclineth unto death, and her paths unto the dead" (Prov. 2:18). "Her feet go down to death; her steps take hold on sheol" (Prov. 5:5). The sense of these passages is not exhausted, by saying that licentiousness leads to physical disease and death. The "death" here threatened is the same that St. Paul speaks of, when he says that "they which commit such things are worthy of death" (Rom. 1:32), and that "the end of those things is death" (Rom.

6 : 21). Eternal death and Sheol are as inseparably joined in Prov. 5 : 5, as eternal death and Hades are in Rev. 20 : 14.

But if Sheol be taken in the mythological sense of an underworld, or spirit-world, there is no inseparable connection between it and "death," either physical or spiritual. Physical death has no power in the spirit-world over a disembodied spirit. And spiritual death is separable from Sheol, in the case of the good. If the good go down to Sheol, they do not go down to eternal death.

II. In the second place, Sheol signifies the "grave," to which all men, the good and evil alike, go down. That Sheol should have the two significations of hell and the grave, is explained by the connection between physical death and eternal retribution. The death of the body is one of the consequences of sin, and an integral part of the penalty. To go down to the grave, is to pay the first instalment of the transgressor's debt to justice. It is, therefore, the metonymy of a part for the whole, when the grave is denominated Sheol. As in English, "death" may mean either physical or spiritual death, so in Hebrew, Sheol may mean either the grave or hell.

When Sheol signifies the "grave," it is only the *body* that goes down to Sheol. But as the body is naturally put for the whole person, the man is said to go down to the grave when his body alone is laid in it. Christ "called Lazarus out of his grave" (John 12 : 17). This does not mean that the soul of Lazarus was in that grave. When a sick person says, "I am going down to the grave," no one understands him to mean that his spirit is descending into a place under the earth. And when the aged Jacob says, "I will go down into sheol, unto my [dead] son mourning" (Gen. 37 : 35), no one should understand him to teach the descent of his disembodied spirit into a subterranean world. "The spirit of man goeth upward, and the spirit of the beast goeth downward" (Eccl. 3 : 21). The soul of the animal dies with the body; that of the man does not. The statement that "the Son of man shall be three days and three nights in the heart of the earth" (Matt. 12 : 40), refers to the burial of his body, not to the residence of his soul.[7] When Christ said to the penitent thief, "To-day shalt thou be with me in paradise," he did not mean that his human soul and that of the penitent should be in "the heart of the earth," but in the heavenly paradise. Christ is represented as dwelling in heaven between his ascension and his second advent. "Him must the heavens receive, till the time of the restitution of all things" (Acts 3 : 21). "The Lord shall descend from heaven with a shout, with the voice of the archangel, and with the trump of God" (1 Thess.

4 : 16). "Our conversation is in heaven, from which we look for our Saviour the Lord Jesus" (Phil. 3 : 20). But the souls of the redeemed, during this same intermediate period, are represented as being with Christ. "Father, I will that they whom thou hast given me be with me where I am, that they may behold my glory which thou hast given me" (John 17 : 24). "We desire rather to be absent from the body, and to be present with the Lord" (2 Cor. 5 : 8). When, therefore, the human body goes down to Sheol, or Hades, it goes down to the grave, and is unaccompanied with the soul.

The following are a few out of many examples of this signification of Sheol. "The Lord killeth, and maketh alive: he bringeth down to sheol, and bringeth up" (1 Sam. 2 : 6). "Thy servants shall bring down the gray hairs of thy servant our father with sorrow to sheol" (Gen. 44 : 31).[8] "O that thou wouldest hide me in sheol" (Job 14 : 13). "Sheol is my house" (Job 17 : 13).[9] Korah and his company "went down alive into sheol, and they perished from the congregation" (Numbers 16 : 33). "In sheol, who shall give thee thanks?" (Ps. 6 : 5). "There is no wisdom in sheol whither thou goest" (Eccl. 9 : 10). "I will ransom them from the power of sheol; O sheol, I will be thy destruction" (Hosea 13 : 14). "My life draweth nigh unto sheol" (Ps. 88 : 3). "What man is he that liveth, and shall not see death? Shall he deliver his soul from the hand of sheol?" (Ps. 89:48). "The English version," says Stuart, "renders Sheol by 'grave' in 30 instances out of 64, and might have so rendered it in more."

Sheol in the sense of the "grave" is invested with gloomy associations for the good, as well as the wicked; and this under the Christian dispensation, as well as under the Jewish. The Old economy and the New are much alike in this respect. The modern Christian believer shrinks from the grave, like the ancient Jewish believer. He needs as much grace in order to die tranquilly, as did Moses and David. It is true that "Christ has brought immortality to light in the gospel;" has poured upon the grave the bright light of his own resurrection, a far brighter light than the Patriarchal and Jewish church enjoyed; yet man's *faith* is as weak and wavering as ever, and requires the support of God.

Accordingly, Sheol in the sense of the "grave" is represented as something out of which the righteous are to be delivered by a resurrection of the body to glory, but the bodies of the wicked are to be left under its power. "Like sheep, the wicked are laid in sheol; death shall feed on them. But God will redeem my soul [me = my body] from the power of sheol" (Ps. 49:14, 15). "Thou wilt not leave my soul [me = my body] in sheol;

neither wilt thou suffer thine Holy One to see corruption" (Ps. 16:10).* This passage, while Messianic, has also its reference to David and all believers. "I will ransom them from the power of sheol. O death, I will be thy plagues; O sheol, I will be thy destruction" (Hosea 13:14). St. Paul quotes this (1 Cor. 15:55), in proof of

* St. Peter (Acts 2:31) asserts that "David spake of the *resurrection* of Christ," when he said that "his soul was not left in sheol, neither did his flesh see corruption." But there is no resurrection of the *soul*. Consequently, it is the body that David "spake of." To "leave Christ's soul in sheol," is the same thing as to "let his flesh see corruption." The uncials, Lachmann, Tischendorf, Hort, and R. V., omit ἡ ψυχὴ αὐτοῦ; and St. Paul (Acts 13:35) omits the clause, "Thou wilt not leave my soul in sheol," evidently regarding the clause, "Thou wilt not suffer thine Holy One to see corruption," as stating the whole fact in the case.

In support of this interpretation of these words, we avail ourselves of the unquestioned learning and accuracy of Bishop Pearson. After remarking that the explanation which makes the clause, "He descended into hell," to mean "that Christ in his body was laid in the grave," is "ordinarily rejected by denying that 'soul' is ever taken for 'body,' or 'hell' for the 'grave,'" he proceeds to say that "this denial is in vain: for it must be acknowledged, that sometimes the Scriptures are rightly so, and cannot otherwise be, understood. First, the same word in the Hebrew, which the Psalmist used, and in the Greek, which the Apostle used, and we translate 'the soul,' is elsewhere used for the body of a dead man, and rendered so in the English version. Both נֶפֶשׁ and ψυχὴ are used for the body of a dead man in the Hebrew, and Septuagint of Num. 6:6: 'He shall come at no dead body' (נֶפֶשׁ מֵת). The same usage is found in Lev. 5:2; 19:28; 21:1, 11; 22:4; Num. 18:11, 13; Haggai 2:13. Thus, several times, נֶפֶשׁ and ψυχὴ are taken for the body of a dead man; that body which polluted a man under the Law, by the touch thereof. And the blessed resurrection of the bodies of believers —showing that "sheol" here is the "grave," where the body is laid, and from which it is raised.

The bodies of the wicked, on the contrary, are not delivered from the power of Sheol, or the grave, by a blessed and glorious resurrection, but

Maimondes hath observed, that there is no pollution from the body till the soul be departed. Therefore נֶפֶשׁ and ψυχή did signify the body after the separation of the soul. And this was anciently observed by St. Augustine, that the soul may be taken for the body only: 'Animæ nomine corpus solum posse significari, modo quodam locutionis ostenditur, quo significatur per id quod continetur illud quod continet' (Epist. 157, al. 190 ad Optatum; De animarum origine, c. 5, § 19). Secondly, the Hebrew word שְׁאוֹל which the Psalmist used, and the Greek word ᾅδης which the Apostle employed, and is translated 'hell' in the English version, doth certainly in some other places signify no more than the 'grave,' and is translated so. As when Mr. Ainsworth followeth the word, 'For I will go down unto my son, mourning, to hell;' our translation, arriving at the sense, rendereth it, 'For I will go down into the grave, unto my son, mourning' (Gen. 37: 35). So again he renders, 'Ye shall bring down my gray hairs with sorrow unto hell,' that is 'to the grave' (Gen. 42: 38). And in this sense we say, 'The Lord killeth and maketh alive: he bringeth down to the grave, and bringeth up' (1 Sam. 2: 6). It is observed by Jewish commentators that those Christians are mistaken who interpret those words spoken by Jacob, 'I will go down into sheol,' of hell [in the sense of underworld]; declaring that Sheol there is nothing but the grave." (Pearson, On the Creed, Article V.) The position that נֶפֶשׁ is sometimes put for a dead body, and that Sheol in such a connection denotes the grave, was also taken by Usher (as it had been by Beza, on Acts 2: 27, before him), and is supported with his remarkable philological and patristic learning. See his discussion of the Limbus Patrum and Christ's

are still kept under its dominion by a "resurrection to shame and everlasting contempt" (Dan. 12:2). Though the wicked are raised from the dead, yet this is no *triumph* for them over death and the grave. Their resurrection bodies are not "celestial" and "glorified," like those of the redeemed, but are suited to the nature of their evil

Descent into Hell, in his Answer to a Challenge of a Jesuit in Ireland (Works, Vol. III.).

This metonymy of "soul" for "body" is as natural an idiom in English, as it is in Hebrew and Greek. It is more easy for one to say that "the ship sank with a hundred souls," than to say that it "sank with a hundred bodies." And yet the latter is the real fact in the case.

It is objected that Sheol does not mean the "grave," because there is a word (קֶבֶר) for grave. A grave is bought and sold, and the plural is used; but Sheol is never bought and sold, or used in the plural. The reply is, that "grave" has an abstract and general sense, denoted by שְׁאוֹל, and a concrete and particular, denoted by קֶבֶר. All men go to the grave; but not all men have a grave. When our Lord says that "all that are in their graves (μνημείοις) shall come forth" (John 5:28), he does not mean that only those shall be raised who have been laid in a particular grave with funeral obsequies. A man is "in the grave," in the general sense, when his soul is separated from his body and his body has "returned to the dust" (Gen. 3:19). To be "in the grave," in the abstract sense, is to have the elements of the body mingled with those of the earth from which it was taken (Eccl. 12:7). The particular spot where the mingling occurs is unessential. Moses is in the grave; but "no man knoweth of his sepulchre unto this day." We say of one drowned in the ocean, that he found a watery grave. These remarks apply also to the use of ᾅδης and μνημεῖον.[10] According to Pearson (ut supra) the Jerusalem Targum, with that of Jonathan, and the Persian Targum, explains שְׁאוֹל, in Gen. 37:35; 42:38, by קֶבֶר.

and malignant souls. "Like sheep they are laid in sheol; death shall feed upon them" (Ps. 49 : 14). Respecting sinful Judah and the enemies of Jehovah, the prophet says, "Sheol hath enlarged herself, and opened her mouth without measure, and their glory shall descend unto it" (Isa. 5 : 14). Of the fallen Babylonian monarch, it is said, "Sheol from beneath is moved for thee to meet thee at thy coming. Thy pomp is brought down to sheol: the worm is spread under thee, and the worms cover thee" (Isa. 14 : 9, 11). To convert this bold personification of the "grave," and the "worm," which devour the bodies of God's adversaries, into an actual underworld, where the spirits of all the dead, the friends as well as the enemies of God, are gathered, is not only to convert rhetoric into logic, but to substitute the mythological for the Biblical view of the future life. "Some interpreters," says Alexander on Isaiah 14: 9, "proceed upon the supposition, that in this passage we have before us not a mere prosopopoeia or poetical creation of the highest order, but a chapter from the popular belief of the Jews, as to the locality, contents, and transactions of the unseen world. Thus Gesenius, in his Lexicon and Commentary, gives a minute topographical description of Sheol as the Hebrews believed it to exist. With equal truth a diligent compiler might construct a map of hell, as conceived by the English Puritans, from the descriptive portions of the Paradise Lost." The clear perception and sound sense of Calvin penetrate more unerringly into the purpose of the sacred writer. "The prophet," he says (Com. on Isa. 14 : 9), "makes a fictitious representation, that when this tyrant shall die and go down to the grave, the dead will go forth to meet him and honor him." Theodoret (Isa. 14 : 9) explains in the same way.[11]

The New Testament terms for the place of future punishment are Hades (ᾅδης) and Gehenna (γέεννα). Besides these, the verb ταρταρόω is once used, in 2 Pet. 2 : 4. "God spared not the angels that sinned, but cast them down to Tartarus." Tartarus was one of the compartments of the pagan Hades, the contrary of Elysium, from which there was no deliverance. Tantalus, Sisyphus, Tityus, and Ixion were doomed to endless punishment in Tartarus (Odyssey, XI. 575). Plato (Gorgias, 235) describes this class of transgressors as "forever (τὸν ἀεὶ χρόνον) enduring the most terrible, and painful sufferings." It is noteworthy, that the place in which they suffer is denominated Hades, by both Homer and Plato—showing that in the classical use, Hades is sometimes the equivalent of Tartarus and the modern Hell, and the contrary of Elysium.

There is no dispute respecting the meaning of Gehenna. It denotes the place of retributive suffering. It is employed twelve times in the New

Testament: seven times in Matthew's Gospel; thrice in Mark's, and once in Luke's. In every one of these instances, it is Christ who uses the term. The only other person who has used it is James (3:6). It is derived from גֵּי הִנֹּם, valley of Hinnom; Chaldee גֵּהִנָּם = Γέεννα, Sept. Ἐννομ. It was a valley southeast of Jerusalem, in which the Moloch worship was practised (2 Kings 23:10; Ezek. 23:37, 39). It was called Tophet, "abomination" (Jer. 31:32). King Josiah caused the filth of Jerusalem to be carried thither and burned (2 Kings 23:10). Robinson asserts that there is no evidence that the place was used in Christ's day for the deposit and burning of offal. "Gehenna," at the time of the Advent, had become a technical term for endless torment; as "Paradise" and "Abraham's bosom" had for endless blessedness; and as "paganus" (villager) subsequently became, for a "heathen."

Hades (ᾅδης) is the word by which the Seventy translate Sheol. It has the same two meanings in the New Testament that Sheol has in the Old: 1. The place of retribution. 2. The grave.

1. First of all, Christ's solemn and impressive parable of Lazarus and Dives demonstrates that Hades is the place of future punishment. "The rich man died and was buried; and in Hades he lifted up his eyes, being in torments. And he cried, and said, Father Abraham have mercy upon me,

and send Lazarus, that he may dip the tip of his finger in water and cool my tongue, for I am tormented in this flame" (Luke 16 : 22–24). Our Lord describes Dives as a disembodied spirit, and as suffering a righteous retribution for his hard-hearted, luxurious, and impenitent life. He had no pity for the suffering poor, and squandered all the "good things received" from his Maker, in a life of sensual enjoyment. The Saviour also represents Hades to be inexorably retributive. Dives asks for a slight mitigation of penal suffering, "a drop of water." He is reminded that he is suffering what he justly deserves, and is told that there is a "fixed gulf" between Hades and Paradise. He then knows that his destiny is decided, and his case hopeless, and requests that his brethren may be warned by his example. After such a description of it as this, it is strange that Hades should ever have been called an abode of the good.[12]

2. Secondly, Hades is represented as the contrary of Heaven, and the contrary of Heaven is Hell. "Thou Capernaum which art exalted unto heaven shalt be brought down to hades" (Matt. 11 : 23; Luke 10 : 15). This is explained by the assertion, that "it shall be more tolerable for the land of Sodom in the day of judgment than for thee."

3. Thirdly, Hades is represented as Satan's kingdom, antagonistic to that of Christ. "The gates of Hades shall not prevail against my

church" (Matt. 16:18). An underworld, containing both the good and the evil, would not be the kingdom of Satan. Satan's kingdom is not so comprehensive as this. Nor would an underworld be the contrary of the church, because it includes Paradise and its inhabitants.

4. Fourthly, Hades is represented as the prison of Satan and the wicked. Christ said to St. John, "I have the keys of Hades and of death" (Rev. 1: 18), and describes himself as "He that openeth, and no man shutteth, and shutteth, and no man openeth" (Rev. 3:7). As the Supreme Judge, Jesus Christ opens and shuts the place of future punishment upon those whom he sentences. "I saw an angel come down from heaven having the key of the bottomless pit, and a great chain in his hand, and he laid hold on the dragon, that old serpent, which is the devil, and Satan, and bound him a thousand years, and cast him into the bottomless pit, and shut him up" (Rev. 20: 1-3). All modifications of the imprisonment and suffering in Hades are determined by Christ. "I saw the dead, small and great, stand before God; and the books were opened, and the dead were judged out of those things which were written in those books; and death and Hades gave up the dead which were in them, and they were judged every man according to their works; and death and Hades were cast into the lake of fire" (Rev. 20:

12–14). On the day of judgment, at the command of the Son of God, Hades, the intermediate state for the wicked, surrenders its inhabitants that they may be re-embodied and receive the final sentence, and then becomes Gehenna, the final state for them. Hell without the body becomes Hell with the body.

5. Fifthly, Hades, like Sheol, is inseparably connected with spiritual and eternal death. "I have the keys of Hades and of death" (Rev. 1 : 18). "Death and Hades gave up the dead which were in them" (Rev. 20 : 13). "I saw a pale horse; and his name that sat upon him was Death, and Hades followed him" (Rev. 6 : 8). Hades here stands for its inhabitants, who are under the power of ("follow") the "second death" spoken of in Rev. 2 : 11; 20 : 6, 14; 21 : 8. This is spiritual and eternal death, and must not be confounded with the first death, which is that of the body only. This latter, St. Paul (1 Cor. 15 : 26) says was "destroyed" by the blessed resurrection of the body, in the case of the saints, not of the wicked. (supra p. 39.) The "second death" is defined as the "being cast into the lake of fire" (Rev. 20 : 14).[13] This "death" is never "destroyed;" because those who are "cast into the lake of fire and brimstone, with the devil that deceived them, shall be tormented day and night for ever and ever" (Rev. 20 : 10).

Besides these instances, there are only three others in which Hades is found in the Received text of the New Testament: namely, Acts 2:27, 31; 1 Cor. 15:55. In 1 Cor. 15:55, the uncials ℵ B C D, followed by Lachmann, Tischendorf, and Hort, read θάνατε twice. In all these instances Hades signifies the "grave."

From this examination of texts, it appears that Hades, in the New Testament, has the same two significations that Sheol has in the Old. The only difference is, that, in the Old Testament, Sheol less often, in proportion to the whole number of instances, denotes "hell," and more often the "grave," than Hades does in the New Testament. And this, for the reason that the doctrine of future retribution was more fully revealed and developed by Christ and his apostles, than it was by Moses and the prophets.

If after this study of the Biblical data, there still be doubt whether Sheol and Hades denote, sometimes the place of retribution for the wicked, and sometimes the grave, and not an under-world, or spirit-world, common to both the good and evil, let the reader substitute either the latter or the former term in the following passages, and say if the connection of thought, or even common sense, is preserved. "The wicked in a moment go down to the spirit-world." "The wicked shall be turned into the spirit-world, and all the nations that forget God." "Her steps take hold on the spirit-world." "Her guests are in the depths of the spirit-world." "Thou shalt beat thy child with a rod, and shalt deliver his soul from the spirit-world." "The way of life is above to the wise, that he may depart from the spirit-world beneath." "In the spirit-world, who shall give thee thanks?" "There is no wisdom in the spirit-world, whither thou goest." "I will ransom them from the power of the spirit-world; O spirit-world I will be thy destruction." "Like sheep the wicked are laid in the spirit-world; death shall feed upon them. But God will redeem my soul from the power of the spirit-world." "Thou wilt not leave my soul in the spirit-world; neither wilt thou suffer thine Holy One to see corruption." "The gates of the spirit-world shall not prevail against the church." "Thou Capernaum which art exalted unto heaven shalt be brought down to the spirit-world." "And in the spirit-world he lift up his eyes being in torments." "Death and the spirit-world were cast into the lake of fire." "I saw a pale horse, and his name that sat upon him was Death, and the spirit-world followed him."

Hades is the *disembodied* state for the souls of the wicked between death and the resurrection, as Paradise is for the souls of the righteous. All human souls between death and the resurrection are separated from their bodies. "Then shall the dust return to the earth as it was; and the spirit shall return to God who gave it" (Eccl. 12: 7).[14] "Jesus, when he had cried again with a loud voice, yielded up the spirit" (Matt. 27: 50). "When Jesus had cried with a loud voice, he said, Father, into thy hands I commend my spirit; and having said this, he gave up the ghost" (Luke 23: 46). "Stephen called upon God, saying, Lord Jesus receive my spirit" (Acts 7: 59). "We are willing rather to be absent from the body, and to be present with the Lord" (2 Cor. 5: 8). "I knew a man in Christ about four years ago, whether in the body or out of the body, I cannot tell" (2 Cor. 12: 2). "I think it meet, as long as I am in this tabernacle, to stir you up by putting you in remembrance: knowing that shortly I must put off this my tabernacle, even as our Lord Jesus Christ hath shewed me" (2 Pet. 1: 13, 14). "I saw the souls of them that were beheaded for the witness of Jesus" (Rev. 20: 4). "I saw under the altar the souls of them that were slain for the word of God" (Rev. 6: 9). All texts which teach the resurrection of the body at the day of judgment, imply that between death and the final judgment the human soul is disembodied.

Belief in the immortality of the soul, and its separate existence from the body after death, was characteristic of the Old economy, as well as the New. It was also a pagan belief. Plato elaborately argues for the difference, as to substance, between the body and the soul, and asserts the independent existence of the latter. He knows nothing of the resurrection of the body, and says that when men are judged, in the next life, "they shall be entirely stripped before they are judged, for they shall be judged when they are dead; and the judge too shall be naked, that is to say, dead; he with his naked soul shall pierce into the other naked soul, as soon as each man dies." (Gorgias 523).

That the independent and separate existence of the soul after death was a belief of the Hebrews, is proved by the prohibition of necromancy in Deut. 18 : 10–12. The "gathering" of the patriarchs "to their fathers" implies the belief. Jehovah calls himself "the God of Abraham, Isaac, and Jacob," and this supposes the immortality and continued existence of their spirits; for, as Christ (Luke 20 : 28) argues in reference to this very point, "God is not the God of the dead, but of the living;" not of the unconscious, but the conscious. Our Lord affirms that the future existence of the soul is so clearly taught by "Moses and the prophets," that if a man is not convinced by them, neither would he be "though one should rise from the dead" (Luke 16 : 29).

Some, like Warburton, have denied that the immortality of the soul is taught in the Old Testament, because there is no direct proposition to this effect, and no proof of the doctrine offered. But this doctrine, like that of the Divine existence, is nowhere formally demonstrated, because it is everywhere assumed. Much of the matter of the Old Testament is nonsense, upon the supposition that the soul dies with the body, and that the sacred writers knew nothing of a future life. For illustration, David says, "My soul panteth after Thee." He could not possibly have uttered these words, if he had expected death to be the extinction of his consciousness. The human soul cannot "pant" for a spiritual communion with God that is to last only seventy years, and then cease forever. Every spiritual desire and aspiration has in it the element of infinity and endlessness. No human being can say to God: "Thou art my God, the strength of my heart, and my portion, for three-score years and ten, and then my God and portion no more forever." When God promised Abraham that in him should "all the families of the earth be blessed" (Gen. 12 : 3), and Abraham "believed in the Lord, and he counted it to him for righteousness" (Gen. 15 : 16), this promise of a Redeemer, and this faith in it, both alike involve a future existence beyond this transitory one. God never would have made such a promise to a creature who was to die with the body; and such a creature could not have trusted in it. In like manner,

Adam could not have believed the protevangelism, knowing that death was to be the extinction of his being. All the Messianic matter of the Old Testament is absurd, on the supposition that the soul is mortal. To redeem from sin a being whose consciousness expires at death, is superfluous. David prays to God, "Take not the word of truth out of my mouth; so shall I keep thy law continually *forever and ever*" (Ps. 119:43, 44). Every prayer to God in the Old Testament implies the immortality of the person praying. "My flesh faileth, but God is the strength of my heart *forever*" (Ps. 63 : 2). "Trust ye in the Lord *forever*, for in the Lord Jehovah is everlasting strength" (Isa. 26 : 4). The nothingness of this life only leads the Psalmist to confide all the more in God, and to expect the next life. "Behold, thou hast made my days as an handbreadth; and mine age is as nothing before thee : verily, every man at his best state is altogether vanity. And now, Lord, what wait I for? my hope is in thee" (Ps. 39: 5, 7). As Sir John Davies says of the soul, in his poem on Immortality :

> "Water in conduit pipes can rise no higher
> Than the well-head from whence it first doth spring :
> Then since to eternal God she doth aspire,
> She cannot be but an eternal thing."

Another reason why the Old Testament contains no formal argument in proof of immortality, and a spiritual world beyond this life, is, because the intercourse with that world on the part of the Old Testament saints and inspired prophets was so immediate and constant. God was not only present to their believing minds and hearts, in his paternal and gracious character, but, in addition to this, he was frequently manifesting himself in theophanies and visions. We should not expect that a person who was continually communing with God would construct arguments to prove his existence; or that one who was brought into contact with the unseen and spiritual world, by supernatural phenomena and messages from it, would take pains to demonstrate that there is such a world. The Old Testament saints "endured as *seeing* the invisible."[15]

The Old Testament teaches the conscious happiness of believers after death. "Enoch walked with God: and he was not; for God took him" (Gen. 5 : 24). "Let me die the death of the righteous, and let my last end be like his" (Numbers 23 : 10). "My flesh shall rest in hope. Thou wilt show me the path of life: in thy presence is fulness of joy" (Ps. 16 : 9, 11). "As for me, I will behold thy face in righteousness: I shall be satisfied when I awake with thy likeness" (Ps. 17 : 15). "God will redeem my soul from the power of the grave; for he shall receive me" (Ps. 49 : 15). "Thou shalt guide me with thy counsel, and afterward receive me to glory. My flesh and my heart faileth; but God is the strength of my heart, and my portion forever" (Ps. 73 : 24, 26). "He will swallow up death in victory; and the Lord God will wipe away tears from all faces" (Isa. 25 : 8). This is quoted by St. Paul (1 Cor. 15 : 54), in proof that "this mortal shall put on immortality." St. Paul also teaches that the Old Testament saints, like those of the New, trusted in the Divine promise of the Redeemer, and of the resurrection. "I stand and am judged for the hope of the promise made of God unto our fathers: unto which promise, our twelve tribes, instantly serving God day and night, hope to come. For which hope's sake, king Agrippa, I am accused of the Jews. Why should it be thought a thing incredible with you, that God should raise the dead?" (Acts 26 : 6–8; comp. 23:6.) "These all died in faith, not having received the promises, but having seen them afar off, and were persuaded of them, and embraced them, and confessed that they were strangers and pilgrims on the earth. For they that say such things declare plainly that they seek a country. And, truly, if they had been mindful of that country from whence they came out, they might have had opportunity to have returned. But now they desire a better country, that is, an heavenly" (Heb. 11 : 13–16). These bright and hopeful anticipations of the Old Testament saints have nothing in common with the pagan world of shades, the gloomy Orcus, where all departed souls are congregated.

The New Testament abundantly teaches the conscious happiness of believers in the disembodied state. "To-day shalt thou be with me in paradise," said Christ to the penitent thief (Luke 23: 43). "They stoned Stephen, calling upon God, and saying, Lord Jesus, receive my spirit" (Acts 7: 59). Immediately on dying, Lazarus is in "Abraham's bosom;" "receives good things;" and is "comforted" (Luke 16 : 23, 25). "To die is gain. I am in a strait betwixt two, having a desire to depart, and be with Christ, which is far better" (Phil. 1 : 21, 23). "I knew a man in Christ, above fourteen years ago, who was caught up to the third heaven, into paradise, and heard unspeakable words, which it is not lawful for a man to utter" (2 Cor. 12 : 2–4). "We know that if our earthly house of this tabernacle were dissolved, we have a building of God; an house not made with hands, eternal in the heavens. Therefore we are always confident, knowing that whilst we are at home in the body we are absent from the Lord. We desire rather to be absent from the body, and to be present with the Lord" (2 Cor. 5:1, 6, 8). "Christ died for us, that, whether we wake or sleep, we should live together with him" (2 Thess. 5 : 10). "I bow my knees unto the Father of our Lord Jesus Christ, of whom the whole family in heaven [not Hades] and earth is named" (Eph. 3:14, 15). "Which hope entereth into that within the veil; whither the forerunner is for us entered, even Jesus" (Heb. 6:20). "And when he had opened the fifth seal, I saw under the altar the souls of them that were slain for the word of God, and white robes were given unto every one of them" (Rev. 6:9, 11). "Blessed are the dead which die in the Lord" (Rev. 14:13).

The doctrine that the condition of all men between death and the resurrection is a *disembodied* condition has been greatly misconceived, and the misconception has introduced errors into eschatology. Inasmuch as the body, though not necessary to personal consciousness, is yet necessary in order to the entire completeness of the person, it came to be supposed in the Patristic church, that the intermediate state is a dubious and unfixed state; that the resurrection adds very considerably both to the holiness and happiness of the redeemed, and to the sinfulness and misery of the lost. This made the intermediate, or disembodied state, to be imperfectly holy and happy for the saved, and imperfectly sinful and miserable for the lost. According to Hagenbach (§ 142), the majority of the fathers between 250 and 730 "believed that men do not receive their full reward till after the resurrection." Jeremy Taylor (Liberty of Prophesying, § 8) asserts that the Latin fathers held that "the saints, though happy, do not enjoy the beatific vision before the resurrection." Even so respectable an authority as Ambrose, the spiritual father of Augustine, taught that the soul "while separated from the body is held in an ambiguous condition" (ambiguo suspenditur).*

The incompleteness arising from the absence of the body was more and more exaggerated in the Patristic church, until it finally resulted in the doctrine of a purgatory for the redeemed, adopted formally by the Papal church, according to which, the believer, between death and the resurrection, goes through a painful process in Hades which

*It is often difficult to say positively, and without qualification, what the opinion of a church father really was upon the subject of Hades, owing to the unsettled state of opinion. One and the same writer, like Tertullian, or Augustine, for example, makes different statements at different times. This accounts for the conflicting representations of dogmatic historians. One thing, however, is certain, that the nearer we approach the days of the Apostles, the less do we hear about an underworld, and of Christ's descent into it. Little is said concerning Hades, by the Apostolical fathers. In the longer recension of Ignatius ad Smyrnæos (Ch. ix.), they are exhorted to "repent while yet there is opportunity, for in Hades no one can confess his sins." Justin Martyr (Trypho, Ch. v.) simply says that "the souls of the pious remain in a better place, while those of the wicked are in a worse, waiting for the time of judgment." The extracts from the fathers in Huidekoper's volume on Christ's Mission to the Underworld, show the uncertainty that prevailed. The same is true of those in König's Christi Höllenfahrt, notwithstanding the bias of the author.[6]

cleanses him from remaining corruption, and fits him for Paradise. The corresponding exaggeration in the other direction, in respect to the condition of the lost in the disembodied state, is found mostly in the Modern church. The Modern Restorationist has converted the intermediate state into one of probation, and redemption, for that part of the human family who are not saved in this life.[17]

The Protestant Reformers, following closely the Scripture data already cited, which represent the redeemed at death as entirely holy and happy in Paradise, and the lost at death as totally sinful and miserable in Hades, rejected altogether the Patristic and Mediæval exaggeration of the corporeal incompleteness of the intermediate state. They affirmed perfect happiness at death for the saved, and utter misery for the lost. The first publication of Calvin was a refutation of the doctrine of the sleep of the soul between death and the resurrection. The Limbus and Purgatory were energetically combated by all classes of Protestants. "I know not," says Calvin (Institutes II. xvi. 9), "how it came to pass that any should imagine a subterraneous cavern, to which they have given the name of limbus. But this fable, although it is maintained by great authors, and even in the present age is by many seriously defended as a truth, is after all nothing but a fable."[18]

The doctrine of the intermediate or disembodied state, as it was generally received in the Reformed (Calvinistic) churches, is contained in the following statements in the Westminster standards: "The souls of believers are, at their *death*, made perfect in holiness, and do immediately pass into glory [The Larger Catechism (86) and Confession (xxxii. 1) say, "into the highest heavens"]; and their bodies, being still united to Christ, do rest in their graves till the resurrection. At the *resurrection*, believers, being raised up in glory, shall be openly acknowledged and acquitted in the day of judgment, and made perfectly blessed in full-enjoying of God to all eternity" (Shorter Catechism, 37, 38). According to this statement, there is no essential difference between Paradise and Heaven. The Larger Catechism (86) asserts that "the souls of the wicked are, at *death*, cast into hell, and their bodies kept in their graves till the resurrection and judgment of the great day." The Larger Catechism (89) and Confession (xxxii. 1) say that "at the *day of judgment*, the wicked shall be cast into hell, to be punished forever." According to this, there is no essential difference between Hades and Hell.

The substance of the Reformed view, then, is, that the intermediate state for the saved is Heaven without the body, and the final state for the saved is Heaven with the body; that the intermediate state for the lost is Hell without the body, and the final state for the lost is Hell with the body. In the Reformed, or Calvinistic eschatology, there is no intermediate Hades between Heaven and Hell, which the good and evil inhabit in common. When this earthly existence is ended, the only specific places and states are Heaven and Hell. Paradise is a part of Heaven; Sheol, or Hades, is a part of Hell. A pagan underworld containing both Paradise and Hades, both the happy and the miserable, like the pagan idol, is "nothing in the world." There is no such place.[19]

This view of Hades did not continue to prevail universally in the Protestant churches. After the creeds of Protestantism had been constructed, in which the Biblical doctrine of Sheol is generally adopted, the mythological view began again to be introduced. Influential writers like Lowth and Herder gave it currency in Great Britain and Germany. "A popular notion," says Lowth (Hebrew Poetry, Lect. VIII.), "prevailed among the Hebrews, as well as among other nations, that the life which succeeded the present was to be passed beneath the earth; and to this notion the sacred prophets were obliged to allude, occasionally, if they wished to be understood by the people, on this subject." Says Herder (Hebrew Poetry, Marsh's Translation, II. 21), "No metaphorical separation of the body and soul was yet known among the Hebrews, as well as among other nations, and the dead were conceived as still living in the grave, but in a shadowy, obscure, and powerless condition." The theory passed to the lexicographers, and many of the lexicons formally defined Sheol and Hades as the underworld. It then went rapidly into commentaries, and popular expositions of Scripture.

The Pagan conception of Hades is wide and comprehensive; the Biblical is narrow and exclusive. The former includes all men; the latter, only wicked men. The Greeks and Romans meant by Hades, neither the grave in which the dead body is laid, nor the exclusive place of retribution, but a nether world in which all departed souls reside. There was one ᾄδης for all, consisting of two subterranean divisions: Elysium and Tartarus.[20] In proportion as the Later-Jews came to be influenced by the Greek and Roman mythology, the Old Testament Sheol was widened, and made to be a region for the good as well as the evil. Usher (Limbus Patrum), and Pearson (Creed, Art. V.), cite Josephus as an example. This mythological influence increased, until the doctrine of purgatory itself came into the Jewish apocryphal literature. Purgatory is taught in 2 Maccabees, 12 : 45. Manasses, in his Prayer, asks God not "to condemn him into the lower parts of the earth." The Synagogue, according to Charnocke (Discourse II.), believed in a purgatory.* [21]

The Pagan conception, as has been observed, passed also into the Christian church. It is found in the writings of many of the fathers, but not in any of the primitive creeds. "The idea of a Hades (שְׁאוֹל), known to both Hebrews and Greeks was transferred to Christianity, and the assumption that the real happiness, or the final misery of the departed, does not commence till after the general judgment and the resurrection of the body, appeared to necessitate the belief in an intermediate state, in which the soul was supposed to remain, from the moment of its separation from the body to the last catastrophe. Tertullian, however, held that the martyrs went at once to paradise, the abode of the blessed, and thought that in this they enjoyed an advantage over other Christians, while Cyprian does not seem to know about any intermediate state whatever" (Hagenbach: History of Doctrine, § 77).[22]

According to this Hellenized eschatology, at death all souls go *down* to Hades: in inferna loca, or ad inferos homines. This is utterly unbiblical. It is connected with the heathen doctrine of the infernal divinities, and the infernal tribunal of Minos and Rhadamanthus. The God of revela-

* On the influence of Hellenism upon the Later-Judaism, see Edersheim's Messianic Prophecy and History. Lecture IX.

tion does not have either his abode, or his judgment-seat, in Hades. From Christ's account of the last judgment, no one would infer that it takes place in an underworld. In both the Old and New Testament, the good dwell with God, and God's dwelling-place is never represented as "below," but "on high." Elijah ascends in a chariot of fire. David expects to be "received to glory." Christ describes the soul of a believer, at death, as going up to Paradise. "The beggar died, and was carried by the angels to Abraham's bosom. The rich man also died, and was buried. And in Hades he lift *up* his eyes, being in torments, and seeth Abraham afar off, and Lazarus in his bosom" (Luke 16:22, 23). According to this description, Abraham's bosom and Hades are as opposite and disconnected as the zenith and the nadir. To say that Abraham's bosom is a part of Hades, is to say that the heavens are a compartment of the earth. St. Matthew (8:11) teaches that Abraham's bosom is in heaven: "Many shall recline (ἀνακλιθήσονται) with Abraham, in the kingdom of heaven." Paradise is separated from Hades by a "great chasm" (Luke 16:26). The word χάσμα denotes space either lateral or vertical, but more commonly the latter. Schleusner, in voce, says: "Maxime dicitur de spatio quod e loco superiore ad inferiorem extenditur." Hades is in infernis; Abraham's bosom, or Paradise, is in superis; and Heaven, proper, is in excelsis, or summis.

If Paradise is a section of Hades, then Christ descended to Paradise, and saints at death go down to Paradise, and at the last day are brought up from Paradise. This difficulty is not met, by resorting to the Later-Jewish distinction between a supernal and an infernal paradise. The paradise spoken of by Christ, in Luke 24:33, is evidently the same that St. Paul speaks of, in 2 Cor. 12:3, 4, which he calls "the third heaven."

It is sometimes said, that there is no "above" or "below" in the spiritual world, and therefore the special representation in the parable of Dives and Lazarus must not be insisted upon. This, certainly, should not be urged by those who contend for an *under*world. Paradise and Hades, like Heaven and Hell, are both in the universe of God. But wherever in this universe they may be, it is the Biblical representation (unlike the mythological), that they do not constitute *one system*, or *one sphere* of being, any more than Heaven and Hell do. They are so contrary and opposite, as to exclude each other, and to constitute two separate places or worlds; so that he who goes to the one does not go to the other. This contrariety and exclusiveness is metaphorically expressed by space vertical, not by space lateral. Things on the same plane are alike. Those on different planes are not. If Paradise is above and Hades is beneath, Hades will be regarded as Hell, and be dreaded. But if Paradise and Hades are both alike beneath, and Paradise is a part of Hades, then Hades will not be regarded as Hell (as some affirm it is not), and will not be dreaded. Hades will be merely a temporary residence of the human soul, where the punishment of sin is imperfect, and its removal possible and probable.

A portion of the fathers, notwithstanding the increasing prevalence of the mythological view, deny that Paradise is a compartment of Hades. In some instances, it must be acknowledged, they are not wholly consistent with themselves, in so doing. According to archbishop Usher (Works, III. 281), "the first who assigned a resting-place in hell [Hades] to the fathers of the Old Testament was Marcion the Gnostic." This was combated, he says, by Origen, in his second Dialogue against Marcion.[23] In his comment on Ps. 9:18, Origen remarks that "as Paradise is the residence of the just, so Hades is the place of punishment (*κολαστήριον*) for sinners." The locating of Paradise in Hades is opposed by Tertullian (Adv. Marcionem, IV. 34), in the following terms: "Hades (inferi) is one thing, in my opinion, and Abraham's bosom is another. Christ, in the parable of Dives, teaches that a great deep is interposed between the two regions. Neither could the rich man have 'lifted up' his eyes, and that too 'afar off,' unless it had been to places above him, and very far above him, by reason of the immense distance between that height and that depth."[24] Similarly, Chrysostom, in his Homilies on Dives and Lazarus, as quoted by Usher, asks and answers: "Why did not Lazarus see the rich man, as well as the rich man is said to see Lazarus? Because he that is in the light does not see him who stands in the dark; but he that is in the dark sees him that is in the light." Augustine, in his exposition of Ps. vi. (Migne, IV. 93), calls attention to the fact that "Dives looked *up*, to see Lazarus." Again, he says, in his Epistle to Evodius (Migne, II. 711), "it is not to be believed that the bosom of Abraham is a part of Hades (aliqua pars inferorum). How Abraham, into whose bosom the beggar was received, could have been in the torments of Hades, I do not understand. Let them explain who can." Again, in De Genesi ad literam, XII. 33, 34 (Migne, III. 482), he remarks: "I confess, I have not yet found that the place where the souls of just men rest is Hades (inferos). If a good conscience may figuratively be called paradise, how much more may that bosom of Abraham, where there is no temptation, and great rest after the griefs of this life, be called paradise." To the same effect, says Gregory of Nyssa (In Pascha. Migne, III. 614): "This should be investigated by the studious, namely, how, at one and the same time, Christ could be in those three places: in the heart of the earth, in paradise with the thief, and in the 'hand' of the Father. For no one will say that paradise is in the places under the earth (ἐν ὑποχθονίοις), or the places under the earth in paradise; or that those infernal places (τὰ ὑποχθόνια) are called the 'hand' of the Father." Cyril of Alexandria, in his De exitu animi (Migne, X. 1079–82), remarks: "Insontes supra, sontes infra. Insontes in cœlo, sontes in profundo. Insontes in manu dei, sontes in manu diaboli." Usher asserts that the following fathers agree with Augustine, in the opinion that Paradise is not in Hades: namely, Chrysostom, Basil, Cyril Alexandrinus, Gregory Nazianzen, Bede, Titus of Bostra, and others.[25]

These patristic statements respecting the supernal locality of Paradise agree with Scripture. "The way of life is *above* to the wise, that he may depart from sheol *beneath*" (Prov. 15:24). When Samuel is represented as coming up from the earth (1 Sam. 28:7–20), it is because the body reanimated rises from the grave. This does not prove that the soul had been in an underworld, any more than the statement of St. John (12:17), that Christ "called Lazarus out of his grave," proves it. Paradise is unquestionably the abode of the saved; and the saved are with Christ. The common residence of both is described as on high. "When he ascended up on high, he led captivity captive" (Eph. 4:8). "Father, I will that they also whom thou hast given me be with me where I am, that they may see my glory" (John 17:24). "Those which sleep in Jesus, God will bring with him" [down from Paradise, not up from Hades] (2 Thess. 4:14). At the second advent, "we which are alive and remain shall be caught up in the clouds, to meet the Lord in the air" (1 Thess. 4:17). Stephen "looked up into heaven, and saw Jesus standing on the right hand of God" (Acts 7:55). Christ said to the Pharisees, "Ye are from beneath, I am from above" (John 8:23). Satan and his angels are "cast down to Tartarus" (2 Pet. 2:4). The penitent thief says to Christ: "Lord remember me when thou comest into thy kingdom." Christ replies: "This day shalt thou be with me in paradise" (Luke 23:42, 43). This implies that paradise is the same as Christ's kingdom; and Christ's kingdom is not an infernal one. Christ "cried with a loud voice, Father into thy hands I commend my spirit, and having said this, he gave up the ghost" (Luke 23:46). The "hands" of the Father, here meant, are in heaven above, not in "sheol beneath."

These teachings of Scripture, and their interpretation by a portion of the fathers, evince that Paradise is a section of Heaven, not of Hades, and are irreconcilable with the doctrine of an under-world containing both the good and the evil.

Another stimulant, besides that of mythology, to the growth of the doctrine that the intermediate state for all souls is the underworld of Hades, was the introduction into the Apostles' creed of the spurious clause, "He descended into Hades." Biblical exegesis is inevitably influenced by the great œcumenical creeds. When the doctrine of the descent to Hades was inserted into the oldest of the Christian symbols, it became necessary to find support for it in Scripture. The texts that can, with any success, be used for this purpose, are few, compared with the large number that prove the undisputed events in the life of Christ. This compelled a strained interpretation of such passages as Matt. 12:40; Acts 2:27; Rom. 10:7; 1 Pet. 3:18–20; 4:6, and largely affected the whole subject of eschatology, as presented in the Scriptures.

The Apostles' creed, in its original form, read as follows: "Suffered under Pontius Pilate; was crucified, dead, and buried; the third day he rose again from the dead." The first appearance of the clause, "He descended into Hades," is in the latter half of the 4th century, in the creed of the church of Aquileia. Pearson (Creed, Art. V.), by citations, shows that the creeds, both ecclesiastical and individual, prior to this time, do not contain it.

Burnet (Thirty Nine Articles, Art. III.) asserts the same. Rufinus, the presbyter of Aquileia, says that the intention of the Aquileian alteration of the creed was, *not to add a new doctrine*, but *to explain an old one;* and therefore the Aquileian creed *omitted* the clause, "was crucified, dead, and buried," and substituted for it the new clause, "descendit in inferna." Rufinus also adds, that "although the preceding Roman and Oriental editions of the creed had not the words, 'He descended into Hades,' yet they had the sense of them in the words, 'He was crucified, dead, and buried,'" (Pearson, Article V.). The early history of the clause, therefore, clearly shows that the "Hades" to which Christ was said to have descended was simply the "grave" in which he was buried.

Subsequently, the clause went into other creeds. The Athanasian (600) follows that of Aquileia, in inserting the "descent" and omitting the "burial." It reads: "Who suffered for our salvation, descended into Hades, rose again the third day from the dead." Those of Toledo, in 633 and 693, likewise contain it. It is almost invariably found in the Mediæval and Modern forms of the Apostles' creed, but *without the omission*, as at first, of the clause, "was crucified, dead, and buried."[26] If, then, the text of the Apostles' creed shall be subjected, like that of the New Testament, to a revision in accordance with the text of the first four centuries, the Descensus ad inferos must be rejected as an interpolation.

While the tenet of Christ's local descent into Hades has no support from Scripture, or any of the first œcumenical creeds, it has support, as has already been observed (p. 56), from patristic authority.* "The ancient fathers," says Pearson (Article V.), "differed much respecting the condition of the dead, and the nature of the place into which the souls, before our Saviour's death, were gathered; some looking on that name which we now translate hell, hades, or infernus, as the common receptacle of the souls of all men, both the just and unjust, while others thought that hades, or infernus, was never taken in the Scriptures for any place of happiness; and therefore they did not conceive the souls of the patriarchs or the prophets did pass into any such infernal place." This difference of opinion appears in Augustine, who wavered in his views upon the subject of Hades, as Bellarmine concedes. Pearson (Art. V.) remarks of him, that "he began to doubt concerning the reason ordinarily given for Christ's descent into hell, namely, to bring up the patriarchs and prophets thence, upon this ground, that he thought the word infernus [ᾅδης] was never taken in Script-

* See Hagenbach's History of Doctrine, §§ 77, 78, 141, 142. Smith's Ed.

ure in a good sense, to denote the abode of the righteous."* Pearson cites, in proof, the passages already quoted from Augustine's Epistles, and Commentary on Genesis. On the other hand, in his City of God (XX. 15), Augustine hesitatingly accepts the doctrine that the Old Testament saints were in limbo, and were delivered by Christ's descent into their abode. "It does not seem absurd to believe, that the ancient saints who believed in Christ, and his future coming, were kept in places far removed, indeed, from the torments of the wicked, but yet in Hades (apud inferos), until Christ's blood and his descent into these places delivered them." Yet in his exposition of the Apostles' creed (De Fide et Symbolo), Augustine makes no allusion to the clause, "He descended into Hades." And the same silence appears in the De Symbolo, attributed to him. After expounding the clauses respecting Christ's passion, crucifixion, and burial, he then explains those concerning his resurrection and ascent into heaven. This proves that when he wrote this exposition, the dogma was not an acknowledged part of the catholic faith.[27] Still later, Peter Chrysologus, archbishop of Ravenna, and Maximus of Turin, explain the

*Notwithstanding the currency which the view of Hades as the abode of the good and evil between death and the resurrection has obtained, it would shock the feelings, should a clergyman say to mourning friends: "Dry your tears, the departed saint has gone down to Hades."

Apostles' creed, and make no exposition of the Descent to Hades. The difference of opinion among the fathers of the first four centuries, together with the absence of Scriptural support for it, is the reason why the Descensus ad inferos was not earlier inserted into the Apostles' creed. It required the development of the doctrine of purgatory, and of the mediæval eschatology generally, in order to get it formally into the doctrinal system of both the Eastern and Western churches.*

The personal and local descent of Christ into Hades—whether to deliver the Old Testament saints from limbo; or to preach judicially, announcing condemnation to the sinners there; or evangelically, offering salvation to them—if a fact, would have been one of the great cardinal facts connected with the Incarnation. It would fall into the same class with the nativity, the baptism, the passion, the crucifixion, the resurrection, and the ascension. Much less important facts than these are recorded. St. Matthew speaks of the descent of Christ into Egypt, but not of his descent into Hades. Such an act of the Redeemer as going down into an infernal world of spirits, would cer-

* Baumgarten-Crusius (Dogmengeschichte II. § 109) finds three stadia in the development of the dogma of the Descent to Hades. 1. The Descent was the Burial itself put into an imaginative form. 2. The Descent was a particular condition or status of Christ resulting from his Burial. 3. The Descent was entirely separate from the Burial, being another and wholly distinct thing.[28]

tainly have been mentioned by some one of the inspired biographers of Christ. The total silence of the four Gospels is fatal to the tenet. St. Paul, in his recapitulation of the principal events of our Lord's life, evidently knows nothing of the descent into Hades. "I delivered unto you that which I also received, how that Christ died for our sins; and that he was buried, and that he rose again the third day" (1 Cor. 15:3, 4). The remark of bishop Burnet (Thirty-Nine Articles, Art. III.) is sound. "Many of the fathers thought that Christ's soul went locally into hell, and preached to some of the spirits there in prison; that there he triumphed over Satan, and spoiled him, and carried some souls with him into glory. But the account that the Scripture gives us of the exaltation of Christ begins it always at his *resurrection*. Nor can it be imagined that so memorable a transaction as this would have been passed over by the first three Evangelists, and least of all by St. John, who coming after the rest, and designing to supply what was wanting in them, and intending particularly to magnify the glory of Christ, could not have passed over so wonderful an instance of it. The passage in St. Peter seems to relate to the preaching to the Gentile world, by virtue of that inspiration that was derived from Christ." *

* Augustine, Bede, Aquinas, Erasmus, Beza, Gerhard, Hottinger, Clericus, Leighton, Pearson, Secker, Hammond, Hofmann, and

Having given the argument from Scripture, in proof that Sheol, Hades, and Gehenna, all denote the place of punishment for the wicked, we proceed to consider the nature and duration of the suffering inflicted in it.

The Old Testament is comparatively silent upon these particulars. Sheol is represented vaguely, as an evil to be dreaded and avoided, and little description of its fearfulness is given by the "holy

most of the Reformed theologians, explain 1 Pet. 3:18–20 to mean, that Christ preached by Noah to men who were "disobedient" in the days of Noah, and who for this cause were "spirits in prison" at the time of Peter's writing.[29] The particle *πότε*, qualifying *ἀπειθήσασί*, shows that the disobedience (or disbelief) occurred "when the ark was a-preparing." But the preaching must have been contemporaneous with the disobedience, or disbelief. What else was there to disobey, or disbelieve? Says Pearson (Creed, Art. II.), "Christ was really before the flood, for he preached to them that lived before it. This is evident from the words of St. Peter (1 Pet. 3:18–20). From which words it appeareth, first, That Christ preached by the same spirit by the virtue of which he was raised from the dead: but that Spirit was not his [human] soul, but something of a greater power; secondly, That those to whom he preached were such as were disobedient; thirdly, That the time when they were disobedient was the time before the flood, when the ark was preparing. The plain interpretation is to be acknowledged for the true, that Christ did preach unto those men which lived before the flood, even while they lived, and consequently that he was before it. For though this was not done by an immediate act of the Son of God, as if he personally had appeared on earth and actually preached to that world, but by the ministry of a prophet, by the sending of Noah, 'the eighth preacher of righteousness:' yet to do anything by another not able to perform it without him, as much demonstrates the exist-

men of old who spake as they were moved by the Holy Ghost." The New Testament makes a fuller revelation and disclosure; and it is principally the Redeemer of the world who widens the outlook into the tremendous future. The suffering in Hades and Gehenna is described as "everlasting (αἰώνιος) punishment" (Matt. 25 : 46); "everlasting (αἰώνιος) fire" (Matt. 18 : 8); "the fire that never shall be quenched" (Mark 9 : 45); "the worm that dieth not" (Mark 9 : 46); "flaming fire" (2 Thess. 1 : 8); "everlasting (ἀΐδίος) chains"

ence of the principal cause, as if he did it himself without any intervening instrument."

Another proof of the correctness of this interpretation is the fact that Christ's preaching to "the spirits in prison" was πνεύματι, alone. The total θεάνθρωπος did not preach. The σάρξ, or human nature, of Christ had no part in the act. But Christ's *personal* and *local* preaching in Hades would require his whole Divine-human person; as much so as his preaching in Galilee or Jerusalem. The Formula Concordiæ (IX. 2) so understands and teaches: "Credimus quod tota persona, deus et homo, post sepulturam, ad inferos descenderit, Satanam devicerit," etc. Christ's preaching through Noah, "a preacher of righteousness" (2 Pet. 2 : 5), and therefore an "ambassador of Christ" (2 Cor. 5 : 20), might be done through his divinity alone. Christ preached πνεύματι through Noah, as David ἐν πνεύματι called him Lord (Matt. 22 : 43). The objection that actually living men upon earth would not be called "spirits" is met by Rom. 13 : 1; 1 John 4 : 1, 3; and by the fact that at the time of Peter's writing the persons meant are disembodied spirits.

The passage 1 Pet. 4 : 6, sometimes cited in proof of the Descensus ad inferos, refers to the preaching of the gospel to the spiritually "dead in trespasses and sins." This is Augustine's interpretation (Ep. ad. Evodium VI. 21). In Eph. 4 : 9, τὰ κατώτερα

(Jude 6); "eternal (αἰώνιος) fire" (Jude 7); "the blackness of darkness forever" (Jude 13); "the smoke of torment ascending up forever and ever" (Rev. 14:11; 19:3); "the lake of fire and brimstone," in which the devil, the beast, and the false prophet "shall be tormented day and night, forever and ever" (Rev. 20:10).

Sensible figures are employed to describe the misery of hell, as they are to describe the blessedness of heaven. It cannot be inferred from the mere use of metaphors, that the duration of either

μέρη τῆς γῆς to which Christ "descended" from "on high" signify this lower world of earth. St. Paul is speaking here of the incarnation. The incarnate Logos did not descend from heaven to hades, nor ascend from hades to heaven. Compare Isa. 44:23: "Shout ye lower parts of the earth." This is the opposite of the "heavens," which are bidden to "sing." In Acts 2:19, this world is called ἡ γῆ κάτω. Hades would be τὰ κατώτατα μέρη τῆς γῆς.[30] In Rom. 10:7, Christ's descent "into the deep" (ἄβυσσον) is shown by the context to be his descent into the grave.

Whatever be the interpretation of 1 Pet. 3:18–20, such a remarkable doctrine as the Descent to Hades should have more foundation than a single disputed text. The doctrine itself is so obscure that it has had five different forms of statement. 1. Christ virtually descended into Hades, because his death was efficacious upon the souls there. 2. Christ actually descended into Hades. 3. Christ's descent into Hades was his suffering the torments of hell. 4. Christ's descent into Hades was his burial in the grave. 5. Christ's descent into Hades was his remaining in the state of the dead, for a season. The Westminster Larger Catechism (50) combines the last two: "Christ's humiliation after his death consisted in his being buried, and continuing in the state of the dead, and under the power of death, till the third day, which hath been otherwise expressed in these words, 'He descended into hell.'"

is temporary. Figures are employed to describe both temporal and eternal realities. The Psalmist describes God as a "rock," a "fortress," a "shield," etc.; and man as a "vapor," a "flower," etc. A figure by its "form," as the rhetoricians call it, indicates the intention of the writer. No one would employ the figure of a rock to denote transiency, or of a cloud to denote permanence. Had Christ intended to teach that future punishment is remedial and temporary, he would have compared it to a dying worm, and not to an undying worm; to a fire that is quenched, and not to an unquenchable fire. The ghost in Hamlet (I. v.) describes the "glow-worm's fire" as "ineffectual," that is, harmless. None of the figures employed in Scripture to describe the misery of the wicked are of the same rhetorical "form" with those of the "morning cloud," the "early dew," etc. They are invariably of the contrary "form," and imply fixedness and immutability. The "smoke of torment" ascends forever and ever. The "worm" of conscience does not die. The "fire" is unquenchable. The "chains" are eternal. The "blackness of darkness" overhangs forever. Had the sacred writers wished to teach that future punishment is for a time only, even a very long time, it would have been easy to have chosen a different species and form of metaphor that would have conveyed their meaning. And if the future punishment of the wicked is not endless, they were morally bound to have avoided conveying the impression they actually have conveyed by the kind of figures they have selected. "It is the wilful deceit," says Paley, "that makes the lie; and we wilfully deceive, when our expressions are not true in the sense in which we believe the hearer to apprehend them."

The epithet *αἰώνιος* ("everlasting") is of prime importance. In order to determine its meaning when applied to the punishment of the wicked, it is necessary, first, to determine that of the substantive from which the adjective is derived. Αἰών signifies an "age." It is a time-word. It denotes "duration," more or less. Of itself, the word "duration," or "age," does not determine the length of the duration, or age. God has duration, and angels have duration. The Creator has an *αἰών*, and the creature has an *αἰών*; but that of the latter is as nothing compared with that of the former. "Behold thou hast made my days as an handbreath; and mine age is as nothing before thee" (Ps. 39 : 5).

In reference to man and his existence, the Scriptures speak of two, and only two *αἰῶνες*, or ages; one finite, and one infinite; one limited, and one endless; the latter succeeding the former.[31] An indefinite series of limited æons with no final endless æon is a Pagan, and Gnostic, not a Biblical conception. The importation of the notion of an endless series of finite cycles, each of which is without finality and immutability, into the Christian system, has introduced error, similarily as the importation of the Pagan conception of Hades has. The misconceiving of a rhetorical figure, in the Scripture use of the plural for the singular, namely, *τοὺς αἰῶνας τῶν αἰώνων* for *τὸν αἰῶνα*, has also contributed to this error.

The two æons, or ages, known in Scripture, are mentioned together in Matt. 12 : 32, "It shall not be forgiven him, neither in this world (*αἰών*), nor in the world (*αἰών*) to come"; in Mark 10 : 30, "He shall receive an hundred-fold now in this time (*καιρός*), and in the world (*αἰών*) to come, eternal life"; in Luke 18:30, "He shall receive manifold more in this present time (*καιρός*), and in the world (*αἰών*) to come, life everlasting"; in Eph. 1:21, "Above every name that is named, not only in this world (*αἰών*), but also in that which is to come." The "things present" and the "things to come," mentioned in Rom. 8 : 38; 1 Cor. 3 : 22, refer to the same two ages. These two æons, or ages, correspond to the two durations of "time" and "eternity," in the common use of these terms. The present age, or æon, is "time;" the future age, or æon, is "eternity."*

* It is relative, not absolute eternity; eternity a parte post, not a parte ante. The future æon, or age, has a beginning, but no ending. This is the meaning, when in common phrase it is said

1. The present finite and limited age, or æon, is denominated in Scripture, "this world" (*ὁ αἰών οὗτος*), עוֹלָם הַזֶּה: Matt. 12 : 32 ; 13 : 22 ; Luke 16 : 8 ; 20 : 34 ; Rom. 12 : 2 ; 1 Cor. 1 : 20 ; 2 : 6, et alia. Another designation is, "this present world" (*ὁ νῦν αἰών*, or *ὁ ἐνεστώς αἰών*): 1 Tim. 6:17; 2 Tim. 4:10; Titus 2 : 12 ; Gal. 1 : 4. Sometimes the present limited age, or æon, is denoted by *αἰών* without the article : Luke 1 : 70, "Which he spake by the mouth of his holy prophets, which have been since the world began" (*ἀπ᾽ αἰῶνος*) ; John 9 : 39, "It was not heard since the world began" (*ἀπ᾽ αἰῶνος*).

For rhetorical effect, the present limited age, or æon, is sometimes represented as composed of a number of lesser ages or cycles, as in modern phrase the sum total of finite earthly time is denominated "the centuries," or "the ages." The following are examples : 1 Cor. 2 : 7, "The hidden wisdom which God ordained before the ages" (*πρό τῶν αἰώνων*). Compare Eph. 3 : 9 ; Col. 1 : 26. In 1 Tim. 1 : 17, God is denominated *βασιλεύς*

that "a man has gone into eternity" ; and that his happiness, or misery, is "eternal." The absolutely eternal has no beginning, as well as no ending ; it is the eternity of God. The relatively eternal has a beginning but no end ; it is the immortality of man and angel. The schoolman called the former, eternitas ; the latter, sempiternitas. Scripture designates the absolute eternity of God, by the phrase, "from everlasting to everlasting" (Ps. 90 : 2). The punishment of the wicked is more properly endless, than eternal.

τῶν αἰώνων, king ot the ages of time, and therefore "the king eternal" (A.V.). In Rom. 16 : 25, a "mystery" is said to have been kept secret *χρόνοις αἰωνίοις*, "during æonian times" (A.V., "since the world began"). The ages of the limited æon are meant. The secret was withheld from all the past cycles of time. In Titus 1 : 2, "eternal life" is said to have been promised *πρό χρόνων αἰωνίων*, "before æonian times" (A.V., "before the world began"). The ages of the limited æon are meant. God promised eternal life, prior to all the periods of time; i.e., eternally promised. In these passages, "æonian times" is equivalent to "the centuries," or the "long ages." The Revisers make the reference to be to the unlimited æon—to eternity, not to time. Their rendering of Titus 1: 2 by, "Before times *eternal*," involves the absurdity that a Divine promise is made prior to eternity; and of Rom. 16 : 25 by, "Through times *eternal*," represents the mystery as concealed during eternity: that is to say, as forever concealed. This rhetorical plural does not destroy the unity of the limited age, or æon. To conceal a mystery from the past "æonian ages," or the past centuries and cycles of finite time, is the same as to conceal it from past finite time as a whole.[32]

2. The future infinite and endless age, or æon, is denominated, in Scripture, "the future world"; A.V. and R.V. "the world to come" (*αἰών ὁ μέλλων*),

עוֹלָם הַבָּא: Matt. 12 : 32; Heb. 2 : 5; 6 : 5. Another designation is, "the world to come" (αἰών ὁ ἐρχόμενος): Mark 10 : 30; Luke 18 : 30. Still another designation is, "*that* world" (αἰών ἐκεῖνος): Luke 20 : 35. Frequently, the infinite and endless age is denoted by αἰών simply, but with the article for emphasis (ὁ αἰών): Mark 3 : 29, "Hath never forgiveness" (εἰσ τὸν αἰώνα); Mt. 51 : 29; John 4 : 14; 6 : 51, 58; 8 : 35, 51, 52; 10 : 28; 11 : 26; 12 : 34; 13 : 8; 14 : 16; 2 Cor. 9 : 9; Heb. 5 : 6; 6 : 20; 7 : 17; 2 Pet. 2 : 17; 1 John 2 : 17; Jude 13.

The same use of the plural for rhetorical effect, employed in the case of the limited æon, is also employed in that of the unlimited. The future infinite αἰών is represented as made up of lesser αἰώνες, or cycles, as, in English, "infinity" is sometimes denominated "the infinities," "eternity," "the eternities," and "immensity," "the immensities." The rhetorical plural, in this instance as in the other, does not conflict with the unity of the infinite age, or æon. The following are examples of this use: Rom. 1 : 25, "The creator is blessed forever" (εἰσ τοὺς αἰῶνας); Rom. 9 : 5; 11 : 36; 16 : 27; 2 Cor. 11 : 31; Phil. 4 : 20; Gal. 1 : 5 (εἰς τοὺς αἰῶνας τῶν αἰώνων); 1 Tim. 1 : 17; Rev. 1 : 6, 18; 4 : 9, 10; 5 : 13; 7 : 12, et alia. The phrases, εἰς τοὺς αἰῶνας, and εἰς τοὺς αἰῶνας τῶν αἰώνων, are equivalent to εἰς τὸν αἰῶνα. All alike denote the one infinite and endless æon, or age.

Since the word æon (αἰών), or age, in Scripture, may denote either the present finite age, or the future endless age, in order to determine the meaning of "æonian" (αἰώνιος), it is necessary first to determine *in which of the two æons*, the limited or the endless, the thing exists to which the epithet is applied; because anything in either æon may be denominated "æonian." The adjective follows its substantive, in meaning. Onesimus, as a slave, existed in this world (αἰών) of "time," and when he is called an æonian, or "everlasting" (αἰώνιος) servant (Philemon 15), it is meant that his servitude continues as long as the finite æon in which he is a servant; and this is practically at an end for him, when he dies and leaves it. The mountains are denominated æonian, or "everlasting" (αἰώνια), in the sense that they endure as long as the finite world (αἰών) of which they are a part endures. God, on the other hand, is a being that exists in the infinite αἰών, and is therefore αἰώνιος in the endless signification of the word. The same is true of the spirits of angels and men, because they exist in the future æon, as well as in the present one. If anything belongs solely to the present age, or æon, it is æonian in the limited signification; if it belongs to the future age, or æon, it is æonian in the unlimited signification. If, therefore, the punishment of the wicked occurs in the *present* æon, it is æonian in the sense of temporal; but if it occurs in the *future* æon, it is æonian in the sense of endless. The adjective takes its meaning from its noun.*

The English word "forever" has the same twofold meaning, both in Scripture and in common use. Sometimes it means as long as a man lives upon earth. The Hebrew servant that had his ear bored with an awl to the door of his master, was to be his servant "forever" (Exod. 21 : 6). Sometimes it means as long as the Jewish state should last. The ceremonial laws were to be statutes "forever" (Lev. 16 : 34). Sometimes it means, as long as the world stands. "One generation passeth away, and another generation cometh; but the earth abideth forever" (Eccl. 1 : 4). In all such instances, "forever" refers to the temporal æon, and denotes finite duration. But in other instances, and they are the great majority in Scripture, "forever" refers to the endless æon; as when it is said that "God is over all blessed forever." The limited signification of "forever" in the former cases, does not disprove its unlimited signification in the latter. That Onesimus was an "everlasting" (*αἰώνιος*) servant, and that the hills are "everlasting" (*αἰώνια*), no more dis-

*"Αἰών de quocunque temporis spatio ita dicitur, ut, quale sit, judicari debeat in singulis locis ex orationis serie et mente scriptoris, rebus adeo et personis, de quibus sermo est." Schleusner, in voce.

proves the everlastingness of God, and the soul; of heaven, and of hell; than the term "forever" in a title deed disproves it. To hold land "forever," is to hold it "as long as grass grows and water runs"—that is, as long as this world, or æon, endures.

The objection that because αἰώνιος, or "æonian," denotes "that which belongs to an age," it cannot mean endless, rests upon the assumption that there is no endless αἰών, or age. It postulates an indefinite series of limited æons, or ages, no one of which is final and everlasting. But the texts that have been cited disprove this. Scripture speaks of but two æons, which cover and include the whole existence of man, and his whole duration. If, therefore, he is an immortal being, one of these must be endless. The phrase "ages of ages," applied to the future endless age, does not prove that there is more than one future age, any more than the phrase "the eternities" proves that there is more than one eternity; or the phrase "the infinities" proves that there is more than one infinity. The plural in these cases is rhetorical and intensive, not arithmetical, in its force.

This examination of the Scripture use of the word αἰώνιος refutes the assertion, that "æonian" means "spiritual" in distinction from "material" or "sensuous," and has no reference at all to time or duration; that when applied to "death," it merely denotes that the death is mental and spiritual in its nature, without saying whether it is long or short, temporary or endless. Beyond dispute, some objects are denominated "æonian," in Scripture, which have nothing mental or spiritual in them. The mountains are "æonian." The truth is, that αἰών is a term that denotes time *only*, and never denotes the nature and quality of an object. All the passages that have been quoted show that duration, either limited or endless, is intended by the word. Whenever this visible world in the sense of the *matter* constituting it is meant, the word employed is κοσμός, and not αἰών. It is only when this world in the sense of the *time* of its continuance is intended, that αἰών is employed. St. Paul, in Eph. 2 : 2, combines both meanings. The heathen, he says, "walk κατὰ τὸν αἰῶνα τõυ κόσμου τούτου—according to the course [duration] of this world [of matter]." In Heb. 1 : 2; 11 : 3, where αἰῶνες denotes the "worlds" created by God, it is, as Lewis (Lange's Ecclesiastes, p. 47) remarks, in opposition to Winer and Robinson, "the time sense, of worlds *after* worlds," not "the space sense, of worlds *beyond* or *above* worlds," that is intended.

In by far the greater number of instances, αἰών and αἰώνιος refer to the future infinite age, and not to the present finite age; to eternity, and not to time. Says Stuart (Exegetical Essays, §§ 13,

16), "*αἰώνιος* is employed 66 times in the New Testament. Of these, 51 relate to the future happiness of the righteous; 7 relate to future punishment: namely, Matt. 18 : 8; 25 : 41, 46; Mark. 3 : 29; 1 Thess. 1 : 9; Heb. 6 : 2; Jude 6; 2 relate to God; 6 are of a miscellaneous nature (5 relating to confessedly endless things, as covenant, invisibilities; and one, in Philemon 15, to a perpetual service). In all the instances in which *αἰώνιος* refers to future duration, it denotes endless duration; saying nothing of the instances in which it refers to future punishment. The Hebrew עוֹלָם is translated in the Septuagint by *αἰών*, 308 times. In almost the whole of these instances, the meaning is, time unlimited; a period without end. In the other instances, it means *αἰών* in the secondary, limited sense; it is applied to the mountains, the Levitical statutes, priesthood, etc." The younger Edwards (Reply to Chauncy Ch. XIV.) says that "*αἰών*, reckoning the reduplications of it, as *αἰῶνες τῶν αἰώνων*, to be single instances of its use, occurs in the New Testament in 104 instances; in 32 of which it means a limited duration. In 7 instances, it may be taken in either the limited or the endless sense. In 65 instances, including 6 instances in which it is applied to future punishment, it plainly signifies an endless duration."

An incidental proof that the adjective *αἰώνιος*

has the unlimited signification when applied to future punishment, is the fact that the destiny of lost men is bound up with that of Satan and his angels. "Then shall he say unto them on the left hand, Depart from me, ye cursed, into everlasting fire, prepared for the devil and his angels" (Matt. 25:41). These are represented in Scripture as hopelessly lost. "The devil that deceived them shall be tormented day and night forever and ever" (Rev. 20:10). The Jews, to whom Christ spoke, understood the perdition of the lost angels to be absolute. If the positions of the Restorationist are true in reference to man, they are also in reference to devils. But Scripture teaches that there is no redemption for the lost angels. "Christ took not on him the nature of angels" (Heb. 2:16).

Respecting the nature of the "everlasting punishment," it is clear from the Biblical representations that it is accompanied with *consciousness*. Dives is "in torments" (Luke 16:23). "The smoke of their torment ascendeth up forever and ever" (Rev. 14:11). "Fear hath torment" (1 John 4:18), and the lost fear "the wrath of the Lamb" (Rev. 6:16). The figures of the "fire," and the "worm" are intended to denote conscious pain. An attempt has been made to prove that the punishment of the wicked is the extinction of consciousness. This doctrine is sometimes denominated Annihilation. Few of its advocates, however, have contended for the strict annihilation of the substance of the soul and body. The more recent defenders maintain the doctrine of Conditional Immortality. According to this view, the soul is not naturally immortal. Some of this class contend that it is material. It gains immortality only through its redemption by Christ. All who are not redeemed, lose all consciousness at the death of the body, and this is the "spiritual death" threatened in Scripture. As the death of the body is the extinction of sensation, so the death of the soul is the extinction of consciousness. The falsity of the theory of Annihilation, in both of its forms, is proved by the following considerations:

1. First, death is the opposite of birth, and birth does not mean the creation of substance. The conception and birth of an individual man, is the uniting of a soul and a body, not the creation ex nihilo of either; and the physical death of an individual man, is the separation of a soul and body, not the annihilation of either. Death is a change of the mode in which a substance exists, and supposes that the substance itself continues in being.

> "Ne, when the life decayes and forme does fade,
> Doth it consume and into nothing goe,
> But chaunged is and often altred to and froe.
> The substaunce is not chaungd nor altred,
> But th' only forme and outward fashion."
>
> Faërie Queene, III. vi.

The death of an animal substance makes an alteration in the relations of certain material atoms, but does not put them out of existence. Dead matter is as far from nonentity as living matter. That physical death is not the annihilation of substance, is proved by 1 Cor. 15 : 36: "That which thou sowest is not quickened except it die." Compare John 12 : 24. In like manner, the death of the soul, or spiritual death, is only a change in the relations of the soul, and its mode of existence, and not the annihilation of its substance. In spiritual death, the soul is separated from God; as in physical death, the soul is separated from the body. The union of the soul with God is spiritual life; its separation from God is spiritual death. "He that hath the Son hath [spiritual] life, and he that hath not the Son hath not [spiritual] life" (1 John 5 : 12).

2. Secondly, the spiritually dead are described in Scripture as conscious. Gen. 2 : 7 compared with Gen. 3 : 8: "In the day thou eatest thereof, thou shalt surely die;" Adam and Eve "hid themselves." After their fall they were spiritually dead, and filled with shame and terror before God. The "dead in trespasses and sins walk according to the course of this world" (Eph. 2 : 1, 2). "She that liveth in pleasure is dead while she liveth" (1 Tim. 5 : 6). "You being dead in your sins hath he forgiven" (Coloss. 2 : 13).

"Thou livest, and art dead" (Rev. 3:1). Spiritual death is the same as the "second death," and the second death "hurts" (Rev. 2:11); and its smoke of torment "ascends forever and ever" (Rev. 19:3).

3. Thirdly, the extinction of consciousness is not of the nature of punishment. The essence of punishment is suffering, and suffering is consciousness. In order to be punished, the person must be conscious of a certain pain, must feel that he deserves it, and know that it is inflicted because he does. All three of these elements are required in a case of punishment. To reduce a man to unconsciousness would make his punishment an impossibility. If God by a positive act extinguishes, at death, the remorse of a hardened villain, by extinguishing his self-consciousness, it is a strange use of language to denominate this a punishment.

Still another proof that the extinction of consciousness is not of the nature of punishment is the fact, that a holy and innocent being might be deprived of consciousness by his Creator, but could not be punished by him. God is not obliged, by his justice, to perpetuate a conscious existence which he originated ex nihilo. For wise ends, he might suffer an unfallen angel not only to lose consciousness, but to lapse into his original nonentity. But he could not, in justice, inflict retributive suffering upon him.

4. Fourthly, the extinction either of being, or of consciousness, admits of no degrees of punishment. All transgressors are "punished" exactly alike. This contradicts Luke 12:47, 48; Rom. 2:12.

5. Fifthly, according to this theory, brutes are punished. In losing consciousness at death, the animal like the man incurs an everlasting loss. The Annihilationist contends that the substance of punishment is in the result, and not in its being felt or experienced. If a transgressor is put out of conscious existence, the result is an everlasting loss to him, though he does not know it. But the same thing is true of a brute. And if the former is punished, the latter is also.

6. Sixthly, the advocate of Conditional Immortality, in teaching that the extinction of consciousness is the "eternal death" of Scripture, implies that the continuance of consciousness is the "eternal life." But mere consciousness is not happiness. Judas was conscious, certainly, when he hung himself, even if he is not now. But he was not happy.

7. Seventhly, the extinction of consciousness is not regarded by sinful men as an evil, but a good. They substitute the doctrine of the eternal sleep of the soul, for that of its eternal punishment. This shows that the two things are not equivalents. When Mirabeau lay dying, he cried passionately

for opium, that he might never awake. The guilty and remorseful have, in all ages, deemed the extinction of consciousness after death to be a blessing; but the advocate of Conditional Immortality explains it to be a curse. "Sight, and hearing, and all earthly good, without justice and virtue," says Plato (Laws II. 661), "are the greatest of evils, *if life be immortal;* but not so great, if the bad man lives a very short time."

8. Eighthly, the fact that the soul depends for its immortality and consciousness upon the upholding power of its Maker does not prove either that it is to be annihilated, or to lose consciousness. Matter also depends for its existence and operations upon the Creator. Both matter and mind can be annihilated by the same Being who created them from nothing. Whether he will cease to uphold any particular work of his hand, can be known only by revelation. In the material world, we see no evidence of such an intention. We are told that "the elements shall melt with fervent heat," but not that they shall be annihilated. And, certainly, all that God has said in Revelation in regard to creation, redemption, and perdition, implies and teaches that he intends to uphold, and not to annihilate the human spirit; to perpetuate, and not extinguish its self-consciousness.

The form of Universalism which is the most

respectable, and therefore the most dangerous, is that which concedes the force of the Biblical and rational arguments respecting the guilt of sin, and its intrinsic desert of everlasting punishment, but contends that redemption from it through the vicarious atonement of Christ is extended into the next world. The advocates of this view assert, that between death and the final judgment the application of Christ's work is going on; that the Holy Spirit is regenerating sinners in the intermediate state, and they are believing and repenting as in this life. This makes the day of judgment, instead of the day of death, the dividing line between "time" and "eternity"; between ὁ *αἰών οὗτος*, and *αἰών ὁ μέλλων*. And this makes the intermediate state a third æon by itself, lying between "time" and "eternity"; between "this world," and "the world to come."

That the "intermediate state" is not a third æon, but a part of the second endless æon, is proved by the following considerations:

1. First, by the fact that in Scripture the disembodied state is not called "intermediate." This is an ecclesiastical term which came in with the doctrine of purgatory, and along with the exaggeration of the difference between Paradise and Heaven, and between Hades and Gehenna.

2. Secondly, by the fact that in Scripture death is represented as the deciding epoch in a man's exist-

ence. It is the boundary between the two Biblical æons, or worlds. Until a man dies, he is in "this world" (ὁ νῦν αἰών); after death, he is in "the future world" (αἰών ὁ μελλων). The common understanding of the teaching of Scripture is, that men are in "time," so long as they live, but when they die, they enter "eternity." "It is appointed unto men once to die, but after that the judgment" (Heb. 9 : 27).[33] This teaches that prior to death, man's destiny is not decided, he being not yet sentenced; but after death, his destiny is settled. When he dies, the "private judgment," that is, the immediate personal consciousness either of penitence or impenitence, occurs. Every human spirit, in that supreme moment when it "returns to God who gave it," knows by direct self-consciousness whether it is a child or an enemy of God, in temper and disposition; whether it is humble and contrite, or proud, hard, and impenitent; whether it welcomes or rejects the Divine mercy in Christ. The article of death is an event in human existence which strips off all disguises, and shows the person what he really is, in moral character. He "knows as he is known," and in this flashing light passes a sentence upon himself that is accurate. This "private judgment" at death, is reaffirmed in the "general judgment" of the last day.

Accordingly, our Lord teaches distinctly that

death is a finality for the impenitent sinner. Twice in succession, he says with awful emphasis to the Pharisees: "If ye believe not that I am he, ye shall die in your sins" (John 8 : 21, 24). This implies, that to "die in sin," is to be hopelessly lost. Again, he says: "Yet a little while is the light with you. Walk while ye have the light, lest darkness come upon you: for he that walketh in darkness knoweth not whither he goeth. While ye have light, believe in the light, that ye may be the children of light" (John 12 : 35, 36). According to these words of the Redeemer, the light of the gospel is not accessible in the darkness of death. "The night cometh, wherein no man can work" (John 9 : 4). The night of death puts a stop to the work of salvation that is appointed to be done in the day-time of this life. St. Paul teaches the same truth, in 1 Thess. 5 : 5–7: "Ye are all the children of light, and the children of the day: we are not of the night, nor of darkness. Therefore let us not sleep, as do others; but let us watch and be sober. For they that sleep, sleep in the night; and they that be drunken, are drunken in the night." "God said unto him, Thou fool, this night thy soul shall be required of thee: then whose shall those things be which thou hast provided? So is he that layeth up treasure for himself, and is not rich towards God" (Luke 12 : 20, 21).

With these New Testament teachings, agrees

the frequent affirmation of the Old Testament, that after death nothing can be done in the way of securing salvation. "In death there is no remembrance of thee: in the grave who shall give thee thanks"? (Ps. 6 : 5). "Wilt thou show wonders to the dead? Shall the dead arise and praise thee? Shall thy loving kindness be declared in the grave"? (Ps. 88 : 10, 11). "The dead praise not the Lord, nor any that go down into silence" (Ps. 115 : 17). "To him that is joined to all the living, there is hope: for the living know that they shall die; but the dead know not anything, neither have they any more a reward" (Eccl. 9 : 4–6). These passages do not teach the utter unconsciousness of the soul after death, in flat contradiction to that long list already cited which asserts the contrary, but that there is no alteration of character in the next life. "In death, there is no [happy] remembrance of God" [if there has been none in life]. "The dead shall not arise, and praise God" [in the next world, if they have not done so in this world]. "Shall God declare his loving kindness [to one] in the grave" [if he has not declared it to him when upon earth]?

The parable of Dives proves that death is the turning point in human existence, and fixes the everlasting state of the person. Dives asks that his brethren may be warned *before* they die and enter Hades; because after death and the entrance into Hades, there is an impassable gulf between misery and happiness, sin and holiness. This shows that the so-called "intermediate" state is not intermediate in respect to the essential elements of heaven and hell, but is a part of the final and endless state of the soul. It is "intermediate," only in reference to the secondary matter of the presence or absence of the body.

The asserted extension of redemption into the endless æon, or age, is contradicted by Scripture. Salvation from sin is represented as confined to the limited æon. One of the most important passages bearing upon this point is 1 Cor. 15 : 24–28. "Then cometh the end, when Christ shall have delivered up the kingdom to God, even the Father, when he shall have put down all [opposing] rule, and all [opposing] authority and power. For he must reign, till he hath put all *enemies* under his feet." St. Paul here states the fact, disclosed to him by revelation from God, that the redemption of sinners will not go on forever, but will cease at a certain point of time. The Mediator will carry on his work of saving sinful men, until he has gathered in his church, and completed the work according to the original plan and covenant between himself and his Father, and then will surrender his mediatorial commission and office (*βασιλείαν*). There will then no longer be any mediation going on between sinners and God.

The church will be forever united to their Divine Head in heaven, and the wicked will be shut up in the "outer darkness." That Christ's mediatorial work does not secure the salvation of all men during the appointed period in which it is carried on, is proved by the fact that when "the end cometh" some men are described as the "enemies" of Christ, and as being "put under his feet" (1 Cor. 15 : 24, 25). All of Christ's redeemed "stand before his throne" (Rev. 14:3; 19: 4-7; 21 : 3). They are in the "mansions" which he has "prepared" for them (John 14 : 2, 3).

The reason assigned for Christ's surrender of his mediatorial commission is, "that *God* may be all in all" (1 Cor. 15 : 28): not, that "God even the *Father* may be all in all" (1 Cor. 15 : 24). It is the Trinity that is to be supreme. To Christ, as an incarnate trinitarian person, and an anointed mediator, "all power is [temporarily] given in heaven and upon earth" (Matt. 28 : 29), for the purpose of saving sinners. As such, he accepts and holds a secondary position of condescension and humiliation, when compared with his original unincarnate position. In this reference, he receives a "commandment" (John 10 : 18), and a "kingdom" (1 Cor. 15 : 24). In this reference, as believers "are Christ's," so "Christ is God's" (1 Cor. 3 : 23); and as "the head of the woman is the man, so the head of Christ is God" (1 Cor. 11: 3).

But when Christ has finished his work of mediating between the triune God and sinful men, and of saving sinners, this condition of subjection to an office and a commission ceases. The dominion (βασιλείαν) over heaven and earth, temporarily delegated to a single trinitarian person incarnate, for purposes of redemption and salvation, now returns to the Eternal Three whence it came, and to whom it originally belongs. The Son of God, his humanity exalted and glorified, and his Divine-human person united forever to his church as their Head, no longer prosecutes that work of redemption which he carried forward through certain ages of time, but, with the Father and Spirit, Three in One, reigns over the entire universe—over the holy "who stand before the throne," and over the wicked who are "under his feet," and "in the bottomless pit."

The confinement of the work of redemption to the limited æon, which terminates practically for each individual at the death of the body, is taught in many other passages of Scripture. "My spirit shall not always [R.V. "for ever"] strive with man, for that he also is [sinful] flesh; yet his days shall be an hundred and twenty years" (Gen. 6:3). This teaches that the converting operation of the Divine Spirit in the sinner's heart, is limited to the 120 years which was to be the average length of human life. "O that they were wise, that they would consider their latter end" (Deut. 32:29). "Teach us so to number our days, that we may apply our hearts unto wisdom" (Ps. 90:12). "Whatsoever thy hand findeth to do, do it with thy might; for there is no work, nor device, nor knowledge, nor wisdom, in the grave whither thou goest" (Eccl. 9:10). "Seek ye the Lord while he may be found; call ye upon him while he is near" (Isa. 55:6). "Take heed to yourselves lest at any time your hearts be overcharged with surfeiting, and drunkenness, and cares of this life, and so that day come upon you unawares: for as a snare shall it come on all them that dwell on the face of the earth" (Luke 21:34, 35). "Watch, therefore, for ye know not what hour your Lord cometh. The Lord of that servant shall come in a day when he looketh not for him, and shall cut him asunder, and appoint him his portion with unbelievers: there shall be weeping and gnashing of teeth" (Mt. 24:42, 50). "If thou hadst known, even thou, at least in this thy day, the things which belong unto thy peace! but now they are hid from thine eyes" (Luke 19:42). "Strive to enter in at the strait gate: for many, I say unto you, will seek to enter in, and shall not be able. When once the master of the house is risen up, and hath shut to the door, and ye begin to stand without, and to knock at the door, saying Lord, Lord, open unto us, he shall answer, and say unto you, I know you not whence ye are" (Luke 13 : 24, 25). "We beseech you that ye receive not the grace of God in vain. For he saith, I have heard thee in a time accepted, and in the day of salvation have I succored thee: behold now is the accepted time; behold now is the day of salvation" (2 Cor. 6 : 2). "To-day if ye will hear his voice, harden not your hearts" (Heb. 3 : 7). The argument in Heb. 3 : 7–19 is to the effect, that as God swore that those Israelites who did not believe and obey his servant Moses during the forty years of wandering in the desert should not enter the earthly Canaan, so those who do not "while it is called, To-day"—that is, while they are here in time—believe and obey his Son Jesus Christ, shall not enter the heavenly Canaan. "Take heed lest there be in any of you an evil heart of unbelief. But exhort one another daily, while it is called, To-day" (Heb. 3 : 12, 13). "God limiteth a certain day, saying in David, To-day, after so long a time [of impenitence], To-day, if ye will hear his voice, harden not your hearts" (Heb. 4 : 7). Hebrews 10 : 26 speaks of a time when "there remaineth no more sacrifice for sins, but a fearful looking-for of judgment and fiery indignation which shall devour the adversaries of God." "Behold I come quickly; and my reward is with me, to give to every man according as his work shall be. He that is unjust, let him be unjust still; and he which is filthy, let him be filthy still; and he that is righteous, let him be righteous still; and he that is holy, let him be holy still" (Rev. 22:11, 12).

If sinners are redeemed beyond the grave, man must be informed of the fact by God himself. There is no other way of finding it out. He has not been so informed, but, if language has any meaning, has been informed of the contrary. Bishop Butler (Analogy, Pt. I. Ch. ii.) states the case with his usual conciseness and clearness. "Reason did, as it well might, conclude that it should finally be well with the righteous, and ill with the wicked; but it could not be determined upon any principles of reason whether human creatures might not have been appointed to pass through other states of life and being, before that distributive justice should finally and effectually take place. Revelation teaches us that the next state of things after the present is appointed for the execution of this justice; that it shall no longer be delayed, but the mystery of God, the great mystery of his *suffering vice and confusion to prevail*, shall then be finished; and he will take to him his great power, and will reign, by rendering to every one according to his works."

The asserted extension of redemption into the period between death and the resurrection cannot be placed upon the ground of right and justice;

and the only other ground possible, that of the Divine promise so to extend it, is wanting. Our Lord teaches that men prior to his coming into the world are "condemned already" (John 3:16). His advent to save them supposes that they are already lost; and they are lost by sin; and sin is man's free self determination.[34] Consequently, man the sinner has no claim upon God for redemption. Forgiveness is undeserved, whether offered here or hereafter. The exercise of mercy is optional with God. "I will have mercy on whom I will have mercy" (Rom. 9:15). It follows from this, that the length of time during which the offer of mercy is made to transgressors is likewise optional with God. It may be long or short, according to the Divine will. Should God say to a sinner: "I will pardon your sin to-day, if you will penitently confess it, but not to-morrow," this sinner could not complain of injustice, but would owe gratitude for the mercy thus extended for a limited time. It cannot be said, that unless God offers to pardon man forever and ever, he is not a merciful Being. Neither can this be said, if he confines redemption to this life, and does not redeem sinners in the intermediate state.*

It is here that the logical inconsistency of such theologians as Müller and Dorner appears. Less-

* Compare the Author's Sermons to the Natural Man. Sermon XVIII.

ing, the first of German critics, makes the following remark respecting the German mind: "We Germans suffer from no lack of systematic books. No nation in the world surpasses us in the faculty of deducing from a couple of definitions whatever conclusions we please, in most fair and logical order." (Preface to the Laocoon.) The truth of this remark is illustrated by some of the systems of theology and philosophy constructed in Germany. The reasoning is close, consecutive, and true, in some sections, but loose, inconsequent, and false, as a whole. The mind of the thinker when moving in the limited sphere, moves logically; but moving in the universe, and attempting to construct a philosophy or theology of the Infinite, fails utterly. Many of the trains of reasoning in Schleiermacher's Glaubenslehre are profound, closely reasoned, and correct, but the system as a whole has fatal defects. No one will deny the rigor of Hegel's logical processes, in segments, but the total circle of his thinking is pantheistic, and full of inconsistency.

Lessing's remark applies to that type of Universalism of which Müller and Dorner are the best representatives, and the ablest advocates. In the first place, upon "a couple" of obscure and dubious scripture texts, they rear the whole great fabric of a future redemption, in direct contradiction to some scores of perfectly plain texts that teach the confinement of redemption to this life And, secondly, after laying down a theory of sin which represents it as pure self-determination and guilt, sin is then discussed as an evil that is entitled to the offer of a pardon, and a remedy. Müller and Dorner, both alike, explain sin as originating in the free and guilty agency of the finite will, and as requiring an atonement in order to its remission.* And yet both alike, when they come to eschatology, assume tacitly, but do not formally assert, that the Divine Perfection requires that the offer of forgiveness be made, sooner or later, to every sinner; that there will be a defect in the benevolence, and a blemish in the character, of the Supreme Being, if he does not tender a pardon to every transgressor of his law. Their eschatology thus contradicts their hamartiology.

The extension of the work of redemption into the future world is made to rest very much, for its support, upon the cases of the heathen and of infants. Respecting the former, it is certain that the heathen are voluntary transgressors of the moral law, and therefore have no claim upon the Divine mercy. Scripture teaches that they perish because of their sin, and impenitence in sin. It is wicked to sin, and still more wicked not to repent

* The merit of Müller, in particular, in respect to a profound and true view of sin is very great. No theological treatise of this century has more value than his work on Sin.

of it. The heathen are chargeable with both. St. Paul describes them as those "who knowing the judgment of God, that they which commit such things are worthy of death, not only do the same, but have pleasure in them that do them" (Rom. 1 : 32). "The Gentiles walk in the vanity of their mind, having the understanding darkened, being alienated from the life of God through the ignorance that is in them, because of the blindness of their heart, who being past feeling have given themselves over unto lasciviousness to work all uncleanness with greediness" (Eph. 4 : 17). "There is no respect of persons with God. For as many as have sinned without [written] law shall also perish without [written] law" (Rom. 2 : 11). "The Gentiles show the work of the law written in their hearts, their conscience bearing witness, and their thoughts accusing, in the day when God shall judge the secrets of men by Jesus Christ" (Rom. 2 : 14, 15). "Remember that ye being in time past Gentiles, were at that time without hope, and without God in the world" (Eph. 2 : 11, 12). "Murderers, whoremongers, and idolaters, shall have their part in the lake of fire and brimstone: which is the second death" (Rev. 21: 8).[35] Jesus Christ said from heaven to Saul of Tarsus, that he had appointed him to be "a minister and witness to the Gentiles, to open their eyes, to turn them from darkness to light, and from the power of Satan unto God, that they may receive forgiveness of sins and inheritance among them that are sanctified by faith" (Acts 26 : 16–18). There is, consequently, no ground for asserting that justice and equity require that the pardon of sins be tendered to the heathen in the next life.

It does not follow, however, that because God is not obliged to offer pardon to the unevangelized heathen, either here or hereafter, therefore no unevangelized heathen are pardoned. The electing mercy of God reaches to the heathen. It is not the doctrine of the Church, that the entire mass of pagans, without exception, have gone down to endless impenitence and death. That some unevangelized men are saved, in the present life, by an extraordinary exercise of redeeming grace in Christ, has been the hope and belief of Christendom. It was the hope and belief of the elder Calvinists, as it is of the later.[36] The Second Helvetic Confession (I. 7), after the remark that the ordinary mode of salvation is by the instrumentality of the written word, adds: "Agnoscimus, interim, deum illuminare posse homines etiam sine externo ministerio, quo et quando velit: id quod ejus potentiæ est." The Westminster Confession (X. 3), after saying that "elect infants dying in infancy are regenerated and saved by Christ through the Spirit, who worketh when and where and how he pleaseth," adds, "so also are all other elect persons [regenerated and saved by Christ through the Spirit] who are incapable of being outwardly called by the ministry of the word." This is commonly understood to refer not merely, or mainly, to idiots and insane persons, but to such of the pagan world as God pleases to regenerate without the use of the written revelation. One of the sternest Calvinists of the 16th century, Zanchius, whose treatise on predestination was translated by Toplady, after remarking that many nations have never had the privilege of hearing the word, says (Ch. IV.) that "it is not indeed improbable that some individuals in these unenlightened countries may belong to the secret election of grace, and the habit of faith may be wrought in them." By the term "habit" (habitus), the elder theologians meant an inward disposition of the heart. The "habit of faith" involves penitence for sin, and the longing for its forgiveness and removal. The "habit of faith" is the broken and contrite heart, which expresses itself in the prayer, "God be merciful to me a sinner." It is certain that the Holy Ghost can produce, if he please, such a disposition and frame of mind in a pagan, without employing, as he commonly does, the written word. The case of the blind man, in John 9:36–38, is an example of the "habit of faith," though produced in this instance through the instrumentality of the written law. "Jesus saith unto him, Dost thou believe on the Son of God? He answered and said, *Who is he*, Lord, that I might believe on him? And Jesus said unto him, Thou hast both seen him, and it is he that talketh with thee. And he said, Lord I believe. And he worshipped him." Here was sorrow for sin, and a desire for redemption from it, wrought in the heart by the Divine Spirit, prior to the actual knowledge of Christ as the Saviour of sinners. The cases of the centurion Cornelius, and the Ethiopian eunuch, are also examples of the "habit of faith." These men, under the teaching of the Spirit, were conscious of sin, and were anxiously inquiring if, and how, it could be forgiven. That there is a class of persons in unevangelized heathendom who are the subjects of gracious influences of this kind, is implied in St. Paul's affirmation, that "they are not all Israel, which are of Israel" (Rom. 9:6); and that "they which are of faith, the same are the children of Abraham" (Gal. 3:7). It is taught also in Matt. 8:11; Luke 13:30: "Many shall come from the east and west, and shall sit down with Abraham, and Isaac, and Jacob, in the kingdom of heaven, but the children of the kingdom [those who have had the written word] shall be cast out. And, behold, there are last which shall be first, and there are first which shall be last." This affirmation of Christ was called out by the "habit of faith," or disposition to believe, in that Gentile centurion, respecting whom he said, "I have not found so great faith, no, not in Israel" (Matt. 8:5–10).[37]

The true reason for hoping that an unevangelized heathen is saved is not that he was virtuous, but that he was penitent. A penitent man is necessarily virtuous; but a virtuous man is not necessarily penitent. Sorrow for sin produces morality; but morality does not produce sorrow for sin. A great error is committed at this point. The Senecas, the Antonines, the Plutarchs, and such like, have been singled out as the hopeful examples in paganism. It is not for man to decide what was the real state of the heart; but the *writings* of these men do not reveal the sense of sin; do not express penitence; do not show a craving for redemption. There is too much egotism, self-consciousness, and self-righteousness in them. The man, judged by his books, is moral, but proud. He is virtuous, but plumes himself upon it. This is not a hopeful characteristic, when we are asking what are the prospects of a human soul, before the bar of God. "To this man will I look, saith the Lord, even to him that is poor, and of a contrite spirit, and trembleth at my word" (Isa. 66:2). "Blessed are the poor in spirit; for theirs is the kingdom of heaven" (Matt. 5:3).

This line of remark holds good in Christendom, as well as in Heathendom. There is a class of men in modern society marked by morality, and lofty self-respect, but by no consciousness of sin, and no confession of it. And judged by New Testament principles, no class of mankind is farther off from the kingdom of heaven. There is no class that scorns the publican's cry, and spurns the atoning blood, with such decision and energy as they. To them, the words of Christ, in a similar case, apply: "The publicans and the harlots go into the kingdom of heaven before you" (Mark 21 : 31). The Magdalen is nearer the Divine Pity than the Pharisee. And upon the same principle, those benighted children of ignorance and barbarism who feel their sin and degradation, and are ready to listen with docility to the missionary when he comes with the tidings of the Infinite Compassion, are nearer to heaven, than the children of a gilded and heartless civilization, who have no moral unrest, and turn a deaf ear to all the overtures of mercy.*

* The passage, "In every nation, he that feareth God and worketh righteousness is accepted with him" (Acts 10 : 35), is often explained as teaching that there are in every nation some who live virtuous and exemplary lives, and upon this ground obtain the rewards and blessedness of the future. This would be salvation by works, which is impossible, according to St. Paul. It is with reference to such an interpretation of this text, that the Westminster Confession (X. 4) asserts, that "men not professing the Christian religion cannot be saved in any other way whatever, be they never so diligent to frame their lives according to the light of nature, and the law of that religion which they do profess."[38] In the pas-

This extraordinary work of the Holy Spirit is mentioned by the Redeemer, to illustrate the sovereignty of God in the exercise of mercy, not to guide his church in their evangelistic labor. His command is, to "preach the gospel to every creature." The extraordinary and "strange" work of God is not a thing for man to expect, and rely upon, either in the kingdom of nature, or of grace. It is his ordinary and established method which is to direct him. The law of missionary effort is, that "faith cometh by hearing, and hearing by the word of God" (Rom. 11:17).

Two errors, therefore, are to be avoided: First, that all men are saved; secondly, that only a few men are saved. Some fifty years ago, Schleiermacher surprised all Lutheran Germany with a defence of the Calvinistic doctrine of election; but the surprise was diminished, when it appeared that he held that God has elected, and will save,

sage above cited, the phrase "fearer of God," and "worker of righteousness," is employed *technically*, by St. Peter, to denote *a man inquiring after the way of salvation*—somewhat as it was among the Jews, to signify a proselyte of the gate (Guericke's Church History, p. 29). This is evident from the fact, that to this "devout" Cornelius who "feared God with all his house" (Acts 10:2), the Apostle preached Christ as the *Saviour of sinners*, "through whose name, whosoever believeth in him shall receive remission of sins," and that Cornelius believed, and was baptized (Acts 10: 36–48). He would not have done this, if he had expected that his "fearing God" and "working righteousness"—in other words, his morality and virtue—would save him.

every human creature without exception. This cannot be squared with Scripture. On the other hand, some Calvinists have represented the number of the reprobated as greater than that of the elect, or equal to it. They found this upon the words of Christ, "Many are called, but few are chosen." But this describes the situation at the time when our Lord spake, and not the final result of his redemptive work. Christ himself, in the days of his flesh, called many, but few responded to the call from his gracious lips. Our Lord's own preaching was not as successful as that of his apostles, and of many of his ministers. This was a part of his humiliation, and sorrow. But when Christ shall have "seen of the travail of his soul," and been "satisfied" with what he has seen; when the whole course of the gospel shall be complete, and shall be surveyed from beginning to end; it will be found that God's elect, or church, is "a great multitude which no man can number, out of *all* nations, and kindreds, and peoples, and tongues," and that their voice is as the voice of many waters, and as the voice of mighty thunderings, saying, "Hallelujah, for the Lord God omnipotent reigneth" (Rev. 7 : 9; 19 : 6). The circle of God's election is a great circle of the heavens, and not that of a treadmill.

Respecting the more difficult case of infants—the Scriptures do not discriminate and except them as a class from the mass of mankind, but involve them in the common sin and condemnation. "Suffer little children to come unto me" [their Redeemer] (Luke 18:16). "The promise [of salvation] is unto you, and to your children" (Acts 2:39). The fall in Adam explains their case. Adopting the Augustino-Calvinistic statement of this fall, it can then be said that infants, like all others of the human family, freely and responsibly "sinned in Adam, and fell with him, in his first transgression" (Westminster Shorter Catechism, 16). This is no more impossible, and no more of a mystery, in the case of infants, than of adults. If it be conceded that the whole race apostatized in Adam, infants are righteously exposed to the punishment of sin, and have no claim upon the Divine mercy. The sin which brings condemnation upon them is original sin, and not actual transgressions. But original sin is the sinful inclination of the will. An infant has a rational soul; this soul has a will; this will is wrongly inclined; and wrong inclination is self-determined and punishable. If sinful inclination in an adult needs to be expiated by the atoning blood of Christ, so does sinful inclination in an infant. Infants, consequently, sustain the very same relation to the mercy of God in Christ that the remainder of the human race do. They need the Divine clemency, like the rest of mankind. The "salvation" of infants supposes their prior damnation. Whoever asserts that an infant is "saved," by implication concedes that it is "lost." The salvation of an infant, like that of an adult, involves the remission and removal of sin, and depends upon the unmerited and optional grace of God. This being so, it cannot be said, that God would treat an infant unjustly, if he did not offer him salvation in the intermediate state. And upon the supposition, now common in the evangelical churches, that all infants dying in infancy, being elect, are "regenerated and saved by Christ through the Spirit, who worketh when, and where, and how he pleaseth" (Westminster Confession, X. 3), there is no need of any such offer.[39]

CHAPTER III.

THE RATIONAL ARGUMENT.

The chief objections to the doctrine of Endless Punishment are not Biblical, but speculative. The great majority of students and exegetes find the tenet in the Hebrew and Greek Scriptures. Davidson, the most learned of English rationalistic critics, explicitly acknowledges that "if a specific sense be attached to words, never-ending misery is enunciated in the Bible. On the presumption that one doctrine is taught, it is the eternity of hell torments. Bad exegesis may attempt to banish it from the New Testament Scriptures, but it is still there, and expositors who wish to get rid of it, as Canon Farrar does, injure the cause they have in view by misrepresentation. It must be allowed that the New Testament record not only makes Christ assert everlasting punishment, but Paul and John. But the question should be looked at from a larger platform than single texts—in the light of God's attributes, and the nature of the soul. The destination of man, and the Creator's infinite goodness, conflicting as they do with everlasting punishment, remove it from the sphere of rational belief. If provision be not made in revelation for a change of moral character after death, it is made in reason. Philosophical considerations must not be set aside even by Scripture" (Last Things, pp. 133, 136, 151).

Consequently, after presenting the Biblical argument, for Endless Punishment, it becomes necessary to present the rational argument for it. So long as the controversy is carried on by an appeal to the Bible, the defender of endless retribution has comparatively an easy task. But when the appeal is made to human feeling and sentiment, or to ratiocination, the demonstration requires more effort. And yet the doctrine is not only Biblical, but rational. It is defensible on the basis of sound ethics and pure reason. Nothing is requisite for its maintenance but the admission of three cardinal truths of theism, namely, that there is a just God; that man has free will; and that sin is voluntary action. If these are denied, there can be no defence of endless punishment—or of any other doctrine, except atheism and its corollaries.

The Bible and all the creeds of Christendom affirm man's free agency in sinning against God. The transgression which is to receive the endless punishment is voluntary. Sin, whether it be inward inclination or outward act, is unforced human agency. This is the uniform premise of Christian theologians of all schools. Endless punishment supposes the liberty of the human will, and is impossible without it. Could a man prove that he is necessitated in his murderous hate, and his murderous act, he would prove, in this very proof, that he ought not to be punished for it, either in time or eternity. Could Satan really convince himself that his moral character is not his own work, but that of God, or of nature, his remorse would cease, and his punishment would end. Self-determination runs parallel with hell.[40]

Guilt, then, is what is punished, and not misfortune. Free and not forced agency is what feels the stroke of justice. What, now, is this stroke? What do law and justice do when they punish? Everything depends upon the right answer to this question. The fallacies and errors of Universalism find their nest and hiding-place at this point. The true definition of punishment detects and excludes them.[41]

Punishment is neither chastisement nor calamity. Men suffer calamity, says Christ, not because they or their parents have sinned, "but that the works of God should be made manifest in them" (John 9 : 3). Chastisement is inflicted in order to develop a good, but imperfect character already formed. "The Lord loveth whom he chasteneth," and "what son is he whom the earthly father chasteneth not?" (Hebrews 11 : 6, 7). Punishment, on the other hand, is retribution, and is not intended to do the work of either calamity or chastisement, but a work of its own. And this work is to vindicate law; to satisfy justice. Punishment, therefore, as distinguished from chastisement, is wholly retrospective in its primary aim. It looks back at what has been done in the past. Its first and great object is requital. A man is hung for murder, principally and before all other reasons, because he has voluntarily transgressed the law forbidding murder. He is not hung from a prospective aim, such as his own moral improvement, or for the purpose of deterring others from committing murder. The remark of the English judge to the horse-thief, in the days when such theft was capitally punished, "You are not hung because you have stolen a horse, but that horses may not be stolen," has never been regarded as eminently judicial. It is true that personal improvement may be one consequence of the infliction of penalty. But the consequence must not be confounded with the purpose. Cum hoc non ergo propter hoc. The criminal may come to see and confess that his crime deserves its punishment, and in genuine unselfish penitence may take sides with the law, approve its retribution, and go into the presence of the Final Judge, relying upon that great atonement which satisfies eternal justice for sin; but even this, the greatest personal benefit of all, is not what is aimed at in man's punishment of the crime of murder. For should there be no such personal benefit as this attending the infliction of the human penalty, the one sufficient reason for inflicting it still holds good, namely, the fact that the law has been violated, and demands the death of the offender for this reason simply and only. "The notion of ill-desert and punishableness," says Kant (Praktische Vernunft, 151. Ed. Rosenkranz), "is necessarily implied in the idea of voluntary transgression; and the idea of punishment excludes that of happiness in all its forms. For though he who inflicts punishment may, it is true, also have a benevolent purpose to produce by the punishment some good effect upon the criminal, yet the punishment must be justified, first of all, as pure and simple requital and retribution: that is, as a kind of suffering that is demanded by the law without any reference to its prospective beneficial consequences; so that even if no moral improvement and no personal advantage should subsequently accrue to the criminal, he must acknowledge that justice has been done to him, and that his experience is exactly conformed to his conduct. In every instance of punishment, properly so called, justice is the very first thing, and constitutes the essence of it. A benevolent purpose and a happy effect, it is true, may be conjoined with punishment; but the criminal cannot claim this as his due, and he has no right to reckon upon it. All that he deserves is punishment, and this is all that he can expect from the law which he has transgressed." These are the words of as penetrating and ethical a thinker as ever lived.*

Neither is it true, that the first and principal aim of punishment, in distinction from chastisement, is the protection of society, and the public good. This, like the personal benefit in the preceding case, is only secondary and incidental. The public good is not a sufficient reason for putting a man to death;† but the satisfaction of law

*Beccaria and Bentham are the principal modern advocates of the contrary theory, viz.: that punishment is founded on utility and expediency. Beccaria's position is, that the standard of crime is the injury which it does to society. He refers exclusively to the public good, and never appeals to the moral sentiment (Penny Cyclopædia, Art. Beccaria). Bentham takes the same view, connecting it with the utilitarian ethics. From these writers, this theory has passed considerably into modern jurisprudence. Austin, a popular writer on law, follows Bentham.

The theory which founds morality upon righteousness, and punishment upon justice, is historical. Plato (Laws, X. 904, 905) held that punishment is righteous and retributive. Cicero (De Legibus, I. 14 sq.) contends that true virtue has regard to essential justice, not to utility. Grotius defines penalty as "the evil of suffering which is inflicted on account of the evil of doing." The great English jurists, Coke, Bacon, Selden, and Blackstone, explain punishment by crime, not by expediency. Kant, Herbart, Stahl, Hartenstein, Rothe, and Woolsey, define punishment as requital for the satisfaction of law and justice (Woolsey's Political Science, Pt. II. Ch. viii.).

†Hence, those who found punishment upon utility, and deny that it is retributive, endeavor to abolish capital punishment. And if their theory of penalty is true, they are right in their endeavor.

is. This view of penalty is most disastrous in its influence, as well as false in its ethics. For if the good of the public is the true reason and object of punishment, the amount of it may be fixed by the end in view. The criminal may be made to suffer more than his crime deserves, if the public welfare, in suppressing this particular kind of crime, requires it. His personal desert and responsibility not being the one sufficient reason for his suffering, he may be made to suffer as much as the public safety requires. It was this theory of penalty that led to the multiplication of capital offences. The prevention of forgery, it was once claimed in England, required that the forger should forfeit his life, and upon the principle that punishment is for the public protection, and not for strict and exact justice, an offence against human property was expiated by human life. Contrary to the Noachic statute, which punishes only murder with death, this statute weighed out man's life-blood against pounds, shillings, and pence. On this theory, the number of capital offences became very numerous, and the criminal code very bloody. So that, in the long run, nothing is kinder than exact justice. It prevents extremes in either direction —either that of indulgence, or that of cruelty.

This theory breaks down, from whatever point it be looked at. Suppose that there were but one person in the universe. If he should transgress the law of God, then, upon the principle of expediency as the ground of penalty, this solitary subject of moral government could not be punished—that is, visited with a suffering that is purely retributive, and not exemplary or corrective. His act has not injured the public, for there is no public. There is no need of his suffering as an example to deter others, for there are no others. But upon the principle of justice, in distinction from expediency, this solitary subject of moral government could be punished.

The vicious ethics of this theory of penalty expresses itself in the demoralizing maxim, "It is better that ten guilty men should escape than that one innocent man should suffer." But this is no more true than the converse, "It is better that ten innocent men should suffer than that one guilty man should escape." It is a choice of equal evil and equal injustice. In either case alike, justice is trampled down. In the first supposed case, there are eleven instances of injustice and wrong; and in the last supposed case, there are likewise eleven instances of injustice and wrong. Unpunished guilt is precisely the same species of evil with punished innocence. To say, therefore, that it is better that ten guilty persons should escape than that one innocent man should suffer, is to say that it is better that there should be ten wrongs than one wrong against justice. The maxim assumes that the punishment of the guilty is not of so much consequence as the immunity of the innocent. But the truth is, that both are equally required by justice.

The theory that punishment is retributive honors human nature, but the theory that it is merely expedient and useful degrades it. If justice be the true ground of penalty, man is treated as a person; but if the public good is the ground, he is treated as a chattel or a thing. When suffering is judicially inflicted because of the intrinsic gravity and real demerit of crime, man's free will and responsibility are recognized and put in the foreground; and these are his highest and distinguishing attributes. The sufficient reason for his suffering is found wholly within his own person, in the exercise of self-determination. He is not seized by the magistrate and made to suffer for a reason extraneous to his own agency, and for the sake of something lying wholly outside of himself—namely, the safety and happiness of others—but because of his own act. He is not handled like a brute or an inanimate thing that may be put to good use; but he is recognized as a free and voluntary person, who is not punished because punishment is expedient and useful, but because it is just and right; not because the public safety requires it, but because he owes it. The dignity of the man himself, founded in his lofty but hazardous endowment of free will, is acknowledged.

Supposing it, now, to be conceded, that future punishment is retributive in its essential nature, it follows that it must be endless from the nature of the case. For, suffering must continue as long as the reason for it continues. In this respect, it is like law, which lasts as long as its reason lasts: ratione cessante, cessat ipsa lex. Suffering that is educational and corrective may come to an end, because moral infirmity, and not guilt, is the reason for its infliction; and moral infirmity may cease to exist. But suffering that is penal can never come to an end, because guilt is the reason for its infliction, and guilt once incurred never ceases to be. The lapse of time does not convert guilt into innocence, as it converts moral infirmity into moral strength; and therefore no time can ever arrive when the guilt of the criminal will cease to deserve and demand its retribution. The reason for retribution to-day is a reason forever. Hence, when God disciplines and educates his children, he causes only a temporary suffering. In this case, "He will not keep his anger forever" (Ps. 103: 9). But when, as the Supreme Judge, he punishes rebellious and guilty subjects of his government, he causes an endless suffering. In this case, "their worm dieth not, and the fire is not quenched" (Mark 9:48).

The real question, therefore, is, whether God ever *punishes*. That he chastises, is not disputed. But does he ever inflict a suffering that is not intended to reform the transgressor, and does not reform him, but is intended simply and only to vindicate law, and satisfy justice, by requiting him for his transgression? Revelation teaches that he does. "Vengeance is mine; I will repay, saith the Lord" (Rom. 12:19). Retribution is here asserted to be a function of the Supreme Being, and his alone. The creature has no right to punish, except as he is authorized by the Infinite Ruler. "The powers that be are ordained of God. The ruler is the minister of God, an avenger to execute wrath upon him that doeth evil" (Rom. 13:1, 4). The power which civil government has to punish crime—the private person having no such power—is only a delegated right from the Source of retribution. Natural religion, as well as revealed, teaches that God inflicts upon the voluntary transgressor of law a suffering that is purely vindicative of law. The pagan sages enunciate the doctrine, and it is mortised into the moral constitution of man, as is proved by his universal fear of retribution. The objection, that a suffering not intended to reform, but to satisfy justice, is cruel and unworthy of God, is refuted by the question of St. Paul: "Is God unrighteous who taketh vengeance? God forbid: for how then shall God judge the world?" (Rom. 3:5, 6). It is impossible either to found or administer a government, in heaven or upon earth, unless the power to punish crime is conceded.

The endlessness of future punishment, then, is implied in the endlessness of guilt and condemnation When a crime is condemned, it is absurd to ask, "How long is it condemned?" The verdict "Guilty for ten days" was Hibernian. Damnation means absolute and everlasting damnation. All suffering in the next life, therefore, of which the sufficient and justifying reason is guilt, must continue as long as the reason continues; and the reason is everlasting. If it be righteous to-day, in God's retributive justice, to smite the transgressor because he violated the law yesterday, it is righteous to do the same thing to-morrow, and the next day, and so on ad infinitum; because the state of the case ad infinitum remains unaltered. The guilt incurred yesterday is a standing and endless fact. What, therefore, guilt legitimates this instant, it legitimates every instant, and forever.

The demand that penal suffering shall stop when it has once begun, is as irrational as the demand that guilt shall stop when it has once begun. The *continuous* nature of guilt necessitates the endlessness of retribution. A man, for illustration, is guilty of profanity to-day. God, we will suppose, immediately begins to cause him to suffer in his mind, as the righteous requital for his transgression of the third commandment. The transgressor immediately begins to feel remorse for his sin. Why, upon principles of justice, should he feel remorse for his profanity to-day, and not feel it to-morrow? Why should he feel it to-morrow, and not feel it a million years hence? Why should he feel it a million years hence, and not feel it forever? At what point should remorse stop? If we suppose the state of the case to be unchanged; if we suppose no penitence for the profanity, and no appropriation of the only atonement that cancels guilt; then the mental suffering which the profanity deserves and experiences now, it always must deserve and experience. The same reasoning will apply to whatever suffering besides remorse enters into the sum-total of future punishment.[42]

Again, the endlessness of punishment follows from the *indivisibility* of guilt. The nature of guilt is such that it cannot be divided up and distributed in parts along a length of time, and be expiated in parts, but is concentrated whole and entire at each and every point of time. The guilt of the sin of profanity does not rest upon the transgressor, one part of it at twelve o'clock, and another part of it at half past twelve, and another part of it at one o'clock, and so on. The *whole* infinite guilt of this act of sin against God lies upon the sinner at each and every instant of time. He is no more guilty of the supposed act, at half past twelve, than at twelve, and equally guilty at both of these instants. Consequently, the *whole* infinite penalty can justly be required at any and every moment of time. Yet the whole penalty cannot be paid at any and every moment, by the suffering of that single moment. The transgressor at any and every point in his endless existence is infinitely guilty, and yet cannot cancel his guilt by what he endures at a particular point. Too long a punishment of guilt is thus an impossibility. The suffering of the criminal can never overtake the crime.[43] And the only way in which justice can approximately obtain its dues, is by a never ceasing infliction. We say approximately, because, tested strictly, the endless suffering of a finite being is not strictly infinite suffering; while the guilt of sin against God is strictly infinite. There is, therefore, no over punishment in endless punishment.*

*It must be remembered, that it is the *degree*, together with the endlessness of suffering, that constitutes the justice of it. We can conceive of an endless suffering that is marked by little intensity in the degree of it. Such, according to Augustine, is the suffering of unbaptized infants (mitissima omnium). It is negative banishment, not positive infliction. An evil that is inflicted in a few hours may be greater than one inflicted in endless time. One day of such torment as that of Satan would be a greater distress, than a slight physical pain lasting forever. The infinite incarnate God suffered more agony in Gethsemane, than the whole finite human race could suffer in endless duration. Consequently, the uniformity in the endlessness must be combined with a variety in the intensity of suffering, in order to adjust the future punishment to the different grades of sin.

It will be objected that, though the guilt and damnation of a crime be endless, it does not follow that the suffering inflicted on account of it must be endless also, even though it be retributive and not reformatory in its intent. A human judge pronounces a theft to be endlessly a theft, and a thief to be endlessly a thief, but he does not sentence the thief to an endless suffering, though he sentences him to a penal suffering. But this objection overlooks the fact that human punishment is only approximate and imperfect, not absolute and perfect like the Divine. It is not adjusted exactly and precisely to the *whole* guilt of the offence, but is more or less modified, first, by not considering its relation to God's honor and majesty; secondly, by human ignorance of the inward motives; and, thirdly, by social expediency. Earthly courts and judges look at the transgression of law with reference only to man's temporal relations, not his eternal. They punish an offence as a crime against the State, not as a sin against God. Neither do they look into the human heart, and estimate crime in its absolute and intrinsic nature, as does the Searcher of Hearts and the Omniscient Judge.* A human tribunal punishes

* "Human laws," says Paley (Moral Philosophy, Bk. I. Ch. iii.), "omit many duties, such as piety to God, bounty to the poor, forgiveness of injuries, education of children, gratitude to benefactors. And they permit, or, which is the same thing, suffer to go

mayhem, we will say, with six months' imprisonment, because it does not take into consideration either the malicious and wicked anger that prompted the maiming, or the dishonor done to the Supreme Being by the transgression of his commandment. But Christ, in the final assize, punishes this offence endlessly, because his All-seeing view includes the sum-total of guilt in the case: namely, the inward wrath, the outward act, and the relation of both to the infinite perfection and adorable majesty of God. The human tribunal does not punish the inward anger at all; the Divine tribunal punishes it with hell fire: "For whosoever shall say to his brother, Thou fool, is in danger of hell fire" (Matt. 5:22). The human tribunal punishes seduction with a pecuniary fine, because it does not take cognizance of the selfish and heartless lust that prompted it, or of the affront offered to that Immaculate Holiness which from Sinai proclaimed, "Thou shalt not commit adultery." But the Divine tribunal punishes seduction with an infinite suffering, because of its more comprehensive and truthful view of the whole transaction. And, in addition to all this imperfection in human punishment, the human tribunal may be influenced by prejudice and selfishness.

unpunished, many crimes, such as luxury, prodigality, caprice in the disposition of property by will, disrespect to parents, and a multitude of similar examples."

> "In the corrupted currents of this world,
> Offence's gilded hand may shove by justice;
> And oft 'tis seen, the wicked prize itself
> Buys out the law. But 'tis not so above.
> There is no shuffling, there the action lies
> In his true nature; and we ourselves compelled
> Even to the teeth and forehead of our faults,
> To give in evidence."—Hamlet, III. iv.

Again, human punishment, unlike the Divine, is variable and inexact, because it is to a considerable extent *reformatory* and *protective.* Human government is not intended to do the work of the Supreme Ruler. The sentence of an earthly judge is not a substitute for that of the last day. Consequently, human punishment need not be marked, even if this were possible, with all that absoluteness and exactness of justice which characterizes the Divine. Justice in the human sphere may be relaxed by expediency. Human punishment may sometimes be more severe, and sometimes less severe, than exact requital demands, but Divine punishment may not be. The retributive element must, indeed, enter into human punishment; for no man may be punished by a human tribunal unless he deserves punishment—unless he is a criminal. But retribution is not the *sole* element when man punishes. Man, while not overlooking the guilt in the case, has some reference to the reformation of the offender, and still more to the protection of society. Here, in time, the transgressor is capable of reformation, and society needs protection. Hence civil expediency and social utility modify exact and strict retribution. For the sake of reforming the criminal, the judge sometimes inflicts a penalty that is less than the real guilt of the offence. For the sake of shielding society, the court sometimes sentences the criminal to a suffering greater than his crime deserves. Human tribunals, also, vary the punishment for the same offence—sometimes punishing forgery capitally, and sometimes not; sometimes sentencing those guilty of the same kind of theft to one year's imprisonment, and sometimes to two.

But the Divine tribunal, in the last great day, is invariably and exactly just, because it is *neither reformatory, nor protective.* In eternity, the sinner is so hardened as to be incorrigible, and heaven is impregnable. Hell, therefore, is not a penitentiary. It is righteous retribution, pure and simple, unmodified by considerations either of utility to the criminal, or of safety to the universe.[44] In the day of final account, penalty will not be unjustly mild for the sake of the transgressor, nor unjustly severe for the sake of society. Christ will not punish incorrigible men and devils (for the two receive the same sentence, and go to the same place, Matt. 25 : 41), for the purpose of reforming them, or of screening the righteous from the wicked, but of satisfying the broken law. His punishment at that time will be nothing but just requital. The Redeemer of men is also the Eternal Judge; the Lamb of God is also the Lion of the tribe of Judah; and his righteous word to wicked and hardened Satan, to wicked and hardened Judas, to wicked and hardened pope Alexander VI., will be: "Vengeance is mine; I will repay. Depart from me, ye cursed, that work iniquity" (Rom. 12:19; Matt. 25:41; 7:23). "The Lord Jesus shall be revealed from heaven, with his mighty angels, in flaming fire, taking vengeance on them that know not God, and that obey not the gospel" (2 Thess. 1:7, 8). The wicked will receive their desert, and reap according as they have sown. The suffering will be unerringly adjusted to the intrinsic guilt: no greater and no less than the sin deserves. "That servant which knew his lord's will [clearly], and did not according to his will, shall be beaten with many stripes; but he that knew not [clearly], and did commit things worthy of stripes, shall be beaten with few stripes. As many as have sinned without [written] law, shall also perish without [written] law; and as many as have sinned under [written] law, shall be judged by the [written] law" (Luke 12:47, 48; Rom. 2:12).

It is because the human court, by reason of its ignorance both of the human heart and the true nature of sin against a spiritual law and a holy

God, cannot do the perfect work of the Divine tribunal, that human laws and penalties are only provisional, and not final. Earthly magistrates are permitted to modify and relax penalty, and pass a sentence which, though adapted to man's earthly circumstances, is not absolute and perfect, and is finally to be revised and made right by the omniscient accuracy of God. The human penalty that approaches nearest to the Divine, is capital punishment. There is more of the purely retributive element in this than in any other. The reformatory element is wanting. And this punishment has a kind of endlessness. Death is a finality. It forever separates the murderer from earthly society, even as future punishment separates forever from the society of God and heaven.

The difference between human and divine punishment is well stated by Paley (Moral Philosophy, Book VI. Ch. ix.): "The proper end of human punishment is not the [exact] satisfaction of justice, but the prevention of crimes. By the satisfaction of justice, I mean the retribution of so much pain for so much guilt; which is the dispensation we expect at the hand of God, and which we are accustomed to consider as the order of things that perfect justice requires. Crimes are not by any government punished in proportion to their [exact] guilt, nor in all cases ought to be so, but in proportion to the difficulty and the necessity of preventing them. The crime must be prevented by some means or other; and consequently whatever means appear necessary to this end, whether they be proportionable to the [exact] guilt of the criminal or not, are adopted rightly. It is in pursuance of the same principle, which pervades indeed the whole system of penal jurisprudence, that the facility with which any species of crime is perpetrated has been generally deemed a reason for aggravating the punishment. This severity would be absurd and unjust, if the [exact] guilt of the offender was the immediate cause and measure of the punishment.

On the other hand, from the justice of God we are taught to look for a gradation of punishment exactly proportioned to the guilt of the offender. When, therefore, in assigning the degrees of human punishment we introduce considerations distinct from that of guilt, and a proportion so varied by external circumstances that equal crimes frequently undergo unequal punishments, or the less crime the greater, it is natural to demand the reason why a different measure of punishment should be expected from God; why that rule which befits the absolute and perfect justice of the deity should not be the rule which ought to be preserved and imitated by human laws. The solution of this difficulty must be sought for, in those peculiar attributes of the Divine nature which distinguish the dispensations of Supreme wisdom from the proceedings of human judicature. A Being whose knowledge penetrates every concealment; from the operation of whose will no act or flight can escape; and in whose hands punishment is sure: such a Being may conduct the moral government of his creation in the best and wisest manner, by pronouncing a law that every crime shall finally receive a punishment proportioned to the guilt which it contains, *abstracted from any foreign consideration whatever*, and may testify his veracity to the spectators of his judgments, by carrying this law into strict execution. But when the care of the public safety is intrusted to men whose authority over their fellow creatures is limited by defects of power and knowledge; from whose utmost vigilance and sagacity the greatest offenders often lie hid; whose wisest precautions and speediest pursuit may be eluded by artifice or concealment; a different necessity, a new rule of proceeding results from the very imperfection of their faculties. In their hands, the uncertainty of punishment must be compensated by the severity. The ease with which crimes are committed or concealed, must be counteracted by additional penalties and increased terrors. The very end for which human government is established requires that its regulations be adapted to the suppression of crimes. This end, whatever it may do in the plans of Infinite Wisdom, does not, in the designation of temporal penalties, always coincide with the proportionate punishment of guilt." Blackstone, also (Com. Book IV., Ch. i.), alludes to the same difference in the following words: "The end, or final cause of human punishments, is not atonement or expiation for the crime committed; for that must be left to the just determination of the Supreme Being."

The argument thus far goes to prove that retribution in distinction from correction, or punishment in distinction from chastisement, is endless from the nature of the case: that is, from the nature of guilt. We pass, now, to prove that it is also rational and right.

1. Endless punishment is rational, in the first place, because it is supported by the human conscience. The sinner's own conscience will "bear witness" and approve of the condemning sentence, "in the day when God shall judge the secrets of men by Jesus Christ" (Rom. 2 : 16). Dives, in the parable, when reminded of the justice of his suffering, is silent. Accordingly, all the evangelical creeds say with the Westminster (Larger Catechism, 89) that "the wicked, upon clear evidence and full conviction of their own consciences, shall have the just sentence of condemnation pronounced against them." If in the great day there are any innocent men who have no accusing consciences,

they will escape hell. We may accommodate St. Paul's words (Rom. 13 : 3, 4), and say: "The final judgment is not a terror to good works, but to evil. Wilt thou, then, not be afraid of the final judgment? Keep the law of God perfectly, without a single slip or failure, inwardly or outwardly, and thou shalt have praise of the same. But if thou do that which is evil, be afraid." But a sentence that is justified by the highest and best part of the human constitution must be founded in reason, justice, and truth. It is absurd to object to a judicial decision that is confirmed by the man's own immediate consciousness of its righteousness.

> "For what, my small philosopher, is hell?
> 'Tis nothing but full knowledge of the truth,
> When truth, resisted long, is sworn our foe:
> And calls eternity to do her right."—YOUNG.

The opponent of endless retribution does not draw his arguments from the impartial conscience, but from the bias of self-love and desire for happiness. His objections are not ethical, but sentimental. They are not seen in the dry light of pure truth and reason, but through the colored medium of self-indulgence and love of ease and sin.

Again, a guilty conscience expects endless punishment. There is in it what the Scripture denominates "the fearful looking-for of judgment, and fiery indignation, which shall devour the adversaries" of God (Hebrews 10 : 27). This is the awful apprehension of an evil that is to last forever; otherwise, it would not be so "fearful." The knowledge that future suffering will one day cease would immediately relieve the apprehension of the sinner. A guilty conscience is in its very nature hopeless. Impenitent men, in their remorse, "sorrow as those who have no hope" (1 Thess. 4 : 13). Unconverted Gentiles "have no hope, and are without God in the world" (Eph. 2 : 12). "The hope of the wicked shall be as the giving up of the ghost" (Job 11 : 20). "The hypocrite's hope shall perish" (Job 8 : 13). Consequently, the great and distinguishing element in hell-torment is despair, a feeling that is impossible in any man or fallen angel who knows that he is finally to be happy forever. Despair results from the endlessness of retribution. No endlessness, no despair.* Natural religion, as well as re-

* "If," says Pearson (Creed, Art. V.), "we should imagine any damned soul to have received an express promise of God, that after ten thousand years he would release him from those torments and make him everlastingly happy, and to have a true faith in that promise and a firm hope of receiving eternal life, we could not say that that man was in the same condition with the rest of the damned, or that he felt all that hell which they were sensible of, or all that pain which was due unto his sins; because hope, and confidence, and relying upon God, would not only mitigate all other pains, but wholly take away the bitter anguish of despair." It is obvious, that if God makes any such promise in his word, either expressly, or by implication, despair is not only impossible

vealed, teaches the despair of some men in the future life. Plato (Gorgias 525), Pindar (Olympia II.), Plutarch (De sera vindicta), describe the punishment of the incorrigibly wicked as eternal and hopeless.

In Scripture, there is no such thing as *eternal* hope. Hope is a characteristic of earth and time only. Here, in this life, all men may hope for forgiveness. "Turn, ye prisoners of hope" (Zech. 9 : 2). "Now is the accepted time; now is the day of salvation" (2 Cor. 6 : 2). But in the next world there is no hope of any kind, because there is either fruition or despair. The Christian's hope is converted into its realization : "For what a man seeth, why doth he yet hope for it?" (Rom. 8 : 24). And the impenitent sinner's hope of heaven is converted into despair. Canon Farrar's phrase "eternal hope" is derived from Pandora's box, not from the Bible. Dante's legend over the portal of hell is the truth : "All hope abandon, ye who enter here." *

to the believer of Scripture, but is a *sin*. No man should despair. And if God does not make any such promise, but man makes it to his fellow sinner, in saying, as Satan did to Eve, "Thou shalt not surely die," and the human promise is believed, the effect will be the same. There will be no despair, until the reckless human falsehood is corrected by the awful demonstration at death.

* The words of Paul, in 1 Cor. 13 : 13, are sometimes cited to prove the eternity of hope, because it "abides." But in this passage, "faith, hope, and charity" are contrasted with the supernatural charismata of chapter 12. These latter are transitory, but

That conscience supports endless retribution, is also evinced by the universality and steadiness of the dread of it. Mankind believe in hell, as they believe in the Divine Existence, by reason of their moral sense. Notwithstanding all the attack made upon the tenet in every generation, by a fraction of every generation, men do not get rid of their fear of future punishment. Skeptics themselves are sometimes distressed by it. But a permanent and general fear among mankind cannot be produced by a mere chimera, or a pure figment of the imagination. Men have no fear of Rhadamanthus, nor can they be made to fear him, because they know that there is no such being. "An idol is nothing in the world" (1 Cor. 8 : 4). But men have "the fearful looking-for of judgment" from the lips of God, ever and always. If the Biblical hell were as much a nonentity as the heathen Atlantis, no one would waste his time in endeavoring to prove its non-existence. What man would seriously construct an argument to demonstrate that there is no such being as Jupiter Ammon, or such an animal as the centaur? The very denial of endless retribution evinces by its spasmodic eager-

the former "abide," because they are essential to the Christian life here upon earth. But in respect to the eternity of "faith," St. Paul teaches that it is converted into "sight" (2 Cor. 5 : 7); and that "hope" is converted into "fruition" (Rom. 8 : 24). Charity is "greater" than faith and hope, because it is not changed into something else, but is eternal.

ness and effort to disprove the tenet, the firmness with which it is intrenched in man's moral constitution. If there really were no hell, absolute indifference toward the notion would long since have been the mood of all mankind, and no arguments, either for or against it, would be constructed.

And finally, the demand, even here upon earth, for the punishment of the intensely and incorrigibly wicked, proves that retribution is grounded in the human conscience. When abominable and satanic sin is temporarily triumphant, as it sometimes has been in the history of the world, men cry out to God for his vengeance to come down. "If there were no God, we should be compelled to invent one," is now a familiar sentiment. "If there were no hell, we should be compelled to invent one," is equally true. When examples of great depravity occur, man cries: "How long, O Lord, how long?" The non-infliction of retribution upon hardened villany and successful cruelty causes anguish in the moral sense. For the expression of it, read the imprecatory psalms and Milton's sonnet on the Massacre in Piedmont.

2. In the second place, endless punishment is rational, because of the endlessness of sin. If the preceding view of the relation of penalty to guilt be correct, endless punishment is just, without bringing the sin of the future world into the account. Man incurs everlasting punishment for

"the things done in his body" (2 Cor. 5 : 10). Christ sentences men to perdition, not for what they are going to do in eternity, but for what they have already done in time. It is not necessary that a man should commit all kinds of sin, or that he should sin a very long time, in order to be a sinner. "Whosoever shall keep the whole law, and yet offend in one point, he is guilty of all" (James 2 : 10). One sin makes guilt, and guilt makes hell.[45]

But while this is so, it is a fact to be observed, that sin is actually being added to sin, in the future life, and the amount of guilt is accumulating. The lost spirit is "treasuring up wrath" (Rom. 2 : 5). Hence, there are degrees in the intensity of endless suffering. The difference in the grade arises from the greater resoluteness of the wicked self-determination, and the greater degree of light that was enjoyed upon earth. He who sins against the moral law as it is drawn out in the Sermon on the Mount, sins more determinedly and desperately than the pagan who sins against the light of nature. There are probably no men in paganism who sin so wilfully and devilishly as some men in Christendom. Profanity, or the blaspheming of God, is a Christian and not a Heathen characteristic.* They are Christian peoples who force

* It is related of Dr. Scudder, that on his return from his mission in India, after a long absence, he was standing on the deck of

opium and rum on helpless pagans. These degrees of sin call for degrees of suffering. And there are degrees in future suffering, because it is infinite in duration only. In intensity, it is finite. Consequently, the lost do not all suffer precisely alike, though all suffer the same length of time. A thing may be infinite in one respect and finite in others. A line may be infinite in length, and not in breadth and depth. A surface may be infinite in length and breadth, and not in depth. And two persons may suffer infinitely in the sense of endlessly, and yet one experience more pain than the other.

The endlessness of sin results, first, from the nature and energy of sinful self-determination. Sin is the creature's act solely. God does not work in the human will when it wills antagonistically to him. Consequently, self-determination to evil is an extremely vehement activity of the will. There is no will so wilful as a wicked will. Sin is stubborn and obstinate in its nature, because it is enmity and rebellion. Hence, wicked will intensifies itself perpetually. Pride, left to itself, increases and never diminishes. Enmity and hatred become more and more satanic. "Sin,"

a steamer, with his son, a youth, when he heard a person using loud and profane language. "See, friend," said the doctor, accosting the swearer, "this boy, my son, was born and brought up in a heathen country, and a land of pagan idolatry; but in all his life he never heard a man blaspheme his Maker until now."

says South, "is the only perpetual motion which has yet been found out, and needs nothing but a beginning to keep it incessantly going on." Upon this important point, Aristotle, in the seventh book of his Ethics, reasons with great truth and impressiveness. He distinguishes between ἀκολασία and ἀκρασία; between strong will to wickedness, and weak self-indulgence. The former is viciousness from deliberation and preference, and implies an intense determination to evil in the man. He goes wrong, not so much from the pull of appetite and passion, as purposely, knowingly, and energetically. He has great strength of will, and he puts it all forth in resolute wickedness. The latter quality is more the absence than the presence of will; it is the weakness and irresolution of a man who has no powerful self-determination of any kind. The condition of the former of these two men, Aristotle regarded as worse than that of the latter. He considered it to be desperate and hopeless. The evil is incurable. Repentance and reformation are impossible to this man; for the wickedness in this instance is not mere appetite; it is a principle; it is cold-blooded and total depravity.

Another reason for the endlessness of sin is the bondage of the sinful will. In the very act of transgressing the law of God, there is a reflex action of the human will upon itself, whereby it becomes unable to perfectly keep that law. Sin is the suicidal action of the human will. A man is not forced to kill himself, but if he does, he cannot bring himself to life again. And a man is not forced to sin, but if he does, he cannot of himself get back where he was before sinning. He cannot get back to innocency, nor can he get back to holiness of heart. The effect of vicious habit in diminishing a man's ability to resist temptation is proverbial. An old and hardened debauchee, like Tiberius or Louis XV., just going into the presence of Infinite Purity, has not so much power of active resistance against the sin that has now ruined him, as the youth has who is just beginning to run that awful career. The truth and fact is, that sin, in and by its own nature and operation, tends to destroy all virtuous force, all holy energy, in any moral being. The excess of will to sin is the same thing as defect of will to holiness. The human will cannot be forced and ruined from without. But if we watch the influence of the will upon itself; the influence of its own wrong decisions, and its own yielding to temptations; we shall find that the voluntary faculty may be ruined from within—may surrender itself with such an absorbing vehemence and totality to appetite, passion, and selfishness, that it becomes unable to reverse itself and overcome its own inclination and self-determination. And yet, from beginning to end, there is no compulsion in this process. The transgressor follows himself alone. He has his own way, and does as he likes. Neither God, nor the world, nor Satan, forces him either to be, or to do, evil. Sin is the most spontaneous of self-motion. But self-motion has consequences as much as any other motion. And moral bondage is one of them. "Whosoever committeth sin is the slave of sin," says Christ (John 8 : 34).

The culmination of this bondage is seen in the next life. The sinful propensity, being allowed to develop unresisted and unchecked, slowly but surely eats out all virtuous force as rust eats out a steel spring, until in the awful end the will becomes all habit, all lust, and all sin. "Sin, when it is finished, bringeth forth death" (James 1 : 15). In the final stage of this process, which commonly is not reached until death, when "the spirit returns unto God who gave it," the guilty free agent reaches that dreadful condition where resistance to evil ceases altogether, and surrender to evil becomes demoniacal. The cravings and hankerings of long-indulged and unresisted sin become organic, and drag the man; and "he goeth after them as an ox goeth to the slaughter, or as a fool to the correction of the stocks, till a dart strike through his liver" (Prov. 7 : 22, 23). For though the will to resist sin may die out of a man, the conscience to condemn it never can. This remains eternally.

And when the process is complete; when the responsible creature, in the abuse of free agency, has perfected his moral ruin; when his will to good is all gone; there remain these two in his immortal spirit: sin and conscience, "brimstone and fire" (Rev. 21:8).

Still another reason for the endlessness of sin, is the fact that rebellious enmity toward law and its Source is not diminished, but increased, by the righteous punishment experienced by the impenitent transgressor. Penal suffering is beneficial only when it is humbly accepted, is acknowledged to be deserved, and is penitently submitted to; when the transgressor says, "Father, I have sinned, and am no more worthy to be called thy son; make me as one of thy hired servants" (Luke 15:18, 19); when, with the penitent thief, he says, "We are in this condemnation justly; for we receive the due reward of our deeds" (Luke 23:41).[46] But when in this life retribution is denied, and jeered at; and when in the next life it is complained of, and resisted, and the arm of hate and defiance is raised against the tribunal; penalty hardens and exasperates. This is impenitence. Such is the temper of Satan; and such is the temper of all who finally become his associates. This explains why there is no repentance in hell, and no meek submission to the Supreme Judge.[47] This is the reason why Dives, the impenitent sensualist, is informed that there is no possible passage from Hades to Paradise, by reason of the "great gulf fixed" between the two; and this is the reason why he asks that Lazarus may be sent to warn his five brethren, "lest they also come into this place of torment," where the request for "a drop of water," a mitigation of punishment, is solemnly refused by the Eternal Arbiter. A state of existence in which there is not the slightest relaxing of penal suffering is no state of probation.

3. In the third place, endless punishment is rational, because sin is an infinite evil; infinite not because committed by an infinite being, but against one.[48] We reason invariably upon this principle. To torture a dumb beast is a crime; to torture a man is a greater crime. To steal from one's own mother is more heinous than to steal from a fellow citizen. The person who transgresses is the same in each instance; but the different worth and dignity of the objects upon whom his action terminates makes the difference in the gravity of the two offences. David's adultery was a finite evil in reference to Uriah, but an infinite evil in reference to God. "Against thee only have I sinned," was the feeling of the sinner in this case. Had the patriarch Joseph yielded, he would have sinned against Pharaoh. But the greatness of the sin as related to the fellow-creature is lost in its enormity as related to the Creator, and his only question is:

"How can I do this great wickedness and sin against God?"[1]

The incarnation and vicarious satisfaction for sin by one of the persons of the Godhead, demonstrates the infinity of the evil. It is incredible that the Eternal Trinity should have submitted to such a stupendous self-sacrifice, to remove a merely finite and temporal evil. The doctrine of Christ's vicarious atonement, logically, stands or falls with that of endless punishment. Historically, it has stood or fallen with it. The incarnation of Almighty God, in order to make the remission of sin possible, is one of the strongest arguments for the eternity and infinity of penal suffering.

The objection that an offense committed in a finite time cannot be an infinite evil, and deserve an infinite suffering, implies that crmie must be measured by the time that was consumed in its perpetration. But even in human punishment, no reference is had to the length of time occupied in the commission of the offense. Murder is committed in an instant, and theft sometimes requires hours. But the former is the greater crime, and receives the greater punishment.

4. In the fourth place, that endless punishment is reasonable, is proved by the preference of the wicked themselves. The unsubmissive, rebellious,

[1] On this point, see Edwards On the Justice of God. Works, IV. 228–229.

defiant, and impenitent spirit prefers hell to heaven. Milton correctly represents Satan as saying: "All good to me becomes bane, and in heaven much worse would be my state"; and, also, as declaring that "it is better to reign in hell than to serve in heaven." This agrees with the Scripture representation, that Judas went "to his own place" (Acts 1:25).

The lost spirits are not forced into a sphere that is unsuited to them. There is no other abode in the universe which they would prefer to that to which they are assigned, because the only other abode is heaven. The meekness, lowliness, sweet submission to God, and love of him, that characterize heaven, are more hateful to Lucifer and his angels, than even the sufferings of hell. The wicked would be no happier in heaven than in hell. The burden and anguish of a guilty conscience, says South, is so insupportable, that some "have done violence to their own lives, and so fled to hell as a sanctuary, and chose damnation as a release." This is illustrated by facts in human life. The thoroughly vicious and ungodly man prefers the license and freedom to sin which he finds in the haunts of vice, to the restraints and purity of Christian society. There is hunger, disease, and wretchedness, in one circle; and there is plenty, health, and happiness, in the other. But he prefers the former. He would rather be in the gambling-house and brothel than in the Christian home. "Those that, notwithstanding all gracious means, live continually in rebellion against God; those that impenitently die in their sins; those that desire to live here forever, that they might enjoy their sweet sins; those that are so hardened and naturalized in their vices, that if they were revived and brought again into this world of temptations, would certainly return to the pleasures of sin; is it not right that their incorrigible obstinacy should be punished forever?" (Bates, On Eternal Judgment, Ch. III.).

The finally lost are not to be conceived of as having faint desires and aspirations for a holy and heavenly state, and as feebly but really inclined to sorrow for their sin, but are kept in hell contrary to their yearning and petition. They are sometimes so described by the opponent of the doctrine, or at least so thought of. There is not a single throb of godly sorrow, or a single pulsation of holy desire, in the lost spirit. The temper toward God in the lost is angry and defiant. "They hate both me and my father," says the Son of God, "without a cause" (John 15:24, 25). Satan and his followers "love darkness rather than light," hell rather than heaven, "because their deeds are evil" (John 3:19). Sin ultimately assumes a fiendish form, and degree. It is pure wickedness without regret or sorrow, and with a delight in evil for evil's sake. There are some men who reach this state of depravity even before they die.[49] They are seen in the callous and cruel voluptuaries portrayed by Tacitus, and the heaven-defying atheists described by St. Simon. They are also depicted in Shakespeare's Iago. The reader knows that Iago is past saving, and deserves everlasting damnation. Impulsively, he cries out with Lodovico: "Where is that viper? bring the villain forth." And then Othello's calmer but deeper feeling becomes his own: "I look down towards his feet—but that's a fable: If that thou be'st a devil, *I* cannot kill thee." The punishment is remitted to the retribution of God.*

*It ought to be noticed, that the "hatred" of Himself, and of his Father, which Christ attributes to "the world" (John 15:18, 19), and which is a distinguishing element in impenitence, does not necessarily imply sensuality and vice. Sin may be wholly intellectual — what St. Paul denominates "spiritual wickedness" (Eph. 6:12). The most profound of Shakespearean critics calls attention to "the passionless character of Iago. It is all will in *intellect*" (Coleridge's Works, IV. 180, Harper's Ed.). The "carnal mind" manifests itself in two ways. The proud spirit of the moralist is one phase of it; the self-indulgent spirit of the voluptuary is the other. The Pharisee represents the first; Dives the last. Both alike confess no *sin*, and implore no *forgiveness*. In illustration of the former, consider the temper of a certain class of intellectual men toward the cross of Christ. They are perhaps austerely moral. By temperament, taste, study, and occupation, they have even an antipathy to sensuality. They "scorn delights, and live laborious days." But present for their acceptance those truths of the New Testament which involve the broken and contrite heart, and their whole inward being rises in vehement recoil. Of the effect of the doctrine of election, Calvin remarks that

5. In the fifth place, that endless punishment is rational, is proved by the history of morals. In the records of human civilization and morality, it is found that that age which is most reckless of law, and most vicious in practice, is the age that has the loosest conception of penalty, and is the most inimical to the doctrine of endless retribution. A virtuous and religious generation adopts sound ethics, and reverently believes that "the Judge of all the earth will do right" (Gen. 18 : 25); that God will not "call evil good, and good evil, nor put darkness for light and light for darkness" (Isa. 5 : 20); and that it is a deadly error to assert with the sated and worn-out sensualist: "All things come alike to all; there is one event to the righteous and the wicked" (Eccl. 9 : 2).

"when the human mind hears of it, its irritation breaks all restraint, and it discovers as serious and violent agitation as if alarmed by the sound of a martial trumpet" (Inst. III. xxii. 1). So, too, when the authoritative demand of Jesus Christ, to confess sin, and beg remission through atoning blood, is made to David Hume, or David Strauss, or John Stuart Mill, none of whom were sensualists, it wakens intense mental hostility. Now without asserting which theory in religion is true, that of the New Testament, or that of the skeptic, is it not clear, that *if* there be another life, and *if* the teaching of the New Testament shall prove to be the absolute truth, the latter person must be classed with the "haters of God"? Will not the temper of this unsensual and intellectual man towards what is found, in the end, to be eternal verity, be as thoroughly of the nature of enmity, as that of the most immoral and hardened debauchee?[60]

The French people, at the close of the last century, were a very demoralized and vicious generation, and there was a very general disbelief and denial of the doctrines of the Divine existence, the immortality of the soul, the freedom of the will, and future retribution. And upon a smaller scale, the same fact is continually repeating itself. Any little circle of business men who are known to deny future rewards and punishments are shunned by those who desire safe investments. The recent uncommon energy of opposition to endless punishment, which started about ten years ago in this country, synchronized with great defalcations and breaches of trust, uncommon corruption in mercantile and political life, and great distrust between man and man. Luxury deadens the moral sense, and luxurious populations do not have the fear of God before their eyes. Hence luxurious ages, and luxurious men, recalcitrate at hell, and "kick against the goads." No theological tenet is more important than eternal retribution to those modern nations which, like England, Germany, and the United States, are growing rapidly in riches, luxury, and earthly power. Without it, they will infallibly go down in that vortex of sensuality and wickedness that swallowed up Babylon and Rome. The bestial and shameless vice of the dissolute rich, that has recently been uncovered in the commercial metropolis of the world, is a powerful argument for the necessity and reality of "the lake which burneth with fire and brimstone."

A single remark remains to be made respecting the extent and scope of hell. It is only a spot in the universe of God. Compared with heaven, hell is narrow and limited. The kingdom of Satan is insignificant in contrast with the kingdom of Christ. In the immense range of God's dominion, good is the rule, and evil is the exception. Sin is a speck upon the infinite azure of eternity; a spot on the sun. Hell is only a corner of the universe. The Gothic etymon (Höhle, Hölle) denotes a covered-up hole. In Scripture, hell is a "pit," a "lake"; not an ocean. It is "bottomless," but not boundless. The Gnostic and Dualistic theories, which make God, and Satan, or the Demiurge, nearly equal in power and dominion, find no support in Revelation. The Bible teaches that there will always be some sin, and some death, in the universe. Some angels and men will forever be the enemies of God.[51] But their number, compared with that of unfallen angels and redeemed men, is small. They are not described in the glowing language and metaphors by which the immensity of the holy and blessed is delineated. "The chariots of God are twenty thousand, and thousands of angels" (Ps. 68: 17). "The Lord came from Sinai, and shined forth from mount Paran, and he came with ten thousands of his saints" (Deut. 22: 2). "The Lord hath prepared his throne in the heavens, and his kingdom ruleth over all" (Ps. 103 : 21). "Thine is the kingdom, and the power, and the glory" (Matt. 6: 13). The Lord Christ "must reign till he hath put all enemies under his feet" (1 Cor. 15 : 25). St. John "heard a voice from heaven as the voice of many waters, and as the voice of a great thunder" (Rev. 14: 1). The New Jerusalem "lieth four square, the length is as large as the breadth; the gates of it shall not be shut at all by day; the kings of the earth do bring their honor into it" (Rev. 21 : 16, 24, 25). The number of the lost spirits is never thus emphasized, and enlarged upon. The brief, stern statement is, that "the fearful and unbelieving shall have their part in the lake that burneth with fire and brimstone" (Rev. 21: 8). No metaphors and amplifications are added, to make the impression of an immense "multitude which no man can number." *

*Calvin, explaining the elect "seven thousand," in Rom. 11 : 4, remarks, that "though this stands for an indefinite number, it was the Lord's design to specify a great multitude. Since, then, the grace of God prevails so much in an extreme state of things, let us not lightly give over to the devil all those whose piety does not openly appear to us." Zuingle thought that all who died in early childhood are regenerated and saved. Edwards (Against Chauncy, Chap. XIV.) denies that it is an article of his faith, that "only a small part of the human race will finally be saved." Hopkins

We have thus briefly presented the rational argument for the most severe and unwelcome of all the tenets of the Christian religion. It must have a foothold in the human reason, or it could not have maintained itself against all the recoil and opposition which it elicits from the human heart. Founded in ethics, in law, and in judicial reason, as well as unquestionably taught by the Author of Christianity, it is no wonder that the doctrine of Eternal Retribution, in spite of selfish prejudices and appeals to human sentiment, has always been a belief of Christendom. From theology and philosophy it has passed into human literature, and is wrought into its finest structures. It makes the solemn substance of the Iliad and the Greek Drama. It pours a sombre light into the brightness and grace of the Æneid. It is the theme of the Inferno, and is presupposed by both of the other parts of the Divine Comedy. The epic of Milton derives from it its awful grandeur. And the greatest of the Shakespearean tragedies sound and stir the depths of the human soul, by their delineation of guilt intrinsic and eternal.

In this discussion, we have purposely brought

(Future State, Section V.) asserts that "there is reason to believe that many more of mankind will be saved than lost; yea, it may be many thousands to one." Hodge (Theology III. 879) says that "we have reason to believe that the number of the finally lost, in comparison with the whole number of the saved, will be very inconsiderable."

into view only the righteousness of Almighty God, as related to the voluntary and responsible action of man. We have set holy justice and disobedient free-will face to face, and drawn the conclusions. This is all that the defender of the doctrine of retribution is strictly concerned with. If he can demonstrate that the principles of eternal rectitude are not in the least degree infringed upon, but are fully maintained, when sin is endlessly punished, he has done all that his problem requires. Whatever is just is beyond all rational attack.

But with the Christian Gospel in his hands, the defender of the Divine justice finds it difficult to be entirely reticent, and say not a word concerning the Divine mercy. Over against God's infinite antagonism and righteous severity toward moral evil, there stands God's infinite pity and desire to forgive. This is realized, not by the high-handed and unprincipled method of pardoning without legal satisfaction of any kind, but by the strange and stupendous method of putting the Eternal Judge in the place of the human criminal; of substituting God's own satisfaction for that due from man. In this vicarious atonement for sin, the Triune God relinquishes no claims of law, and waives no rights of justice. The sinner's Divine Substitute, in his hour of voluntary agony and death, drinks the cup of punitive and inexorable justice to the dregs. Any man who, in penitent faith, avails himself of this *vicarious* method of setting himself right with the Eternal Nemesis, will find that it succeeds; but he who rejects it, must through endless cycles grapple with the dread problem of human guilt in his own person, and alone.

The Christian Gospel—the universal offer of pardon through the self-sacrifice of one of the Divine Persons—should silence every objection to the doctrine of Endless Punishment. For as the case now stands, there is no necessity, so far as the action of *God* is concerned, that a single human being should ever be the subject of future punishment. The necessity of hell is founded in the action of the *creature*, not of the Creator. Had there been no sin, there would have been no hell; and sin is the product of man's free will. And after the entrance of sin, and the provision of redemption from it, had there been universal repentance in this life, there would have been no hell for man in the next life. The only necessitating reason, therefore, for endless retribution, that now exists, is the sinner's *impenitence*. Should every human individual, before he dies, sorrow for sin, and humbly confess it, Hades and Gehenna would disappear.

For the Scriptures everywhere describe God as naturally and spontaneously merciful, and declare that all the legal obstacles to the exercise of this great attribute have been removed by the death of the Son of God "for the sins of the whole world" (1 John 2 : 2). In the very midst of the holy revelations of Sinai, Jehovah proclaimed it to be his inherent and intrinsic disposition to be "merciful and gracious, long suffering, forgiving iniquity and transgression" (Ex. 34 : 6, 7). Nehemiah, after the exile, repeats the doctrine of the Pentateuch: "Thou art a God ready to pardon, gracious and merciful, and of great kindness" (Nehem. 9 : 17). The Psalmist declares that "the Lord is ready to forgive, and plenteous in mercy unto all that call upon him" (Ps. 86 : 5). The Bible, throughout, teaches that the Supreme Being is tenderly sensitive to penitence, and is moved with compassion and paternal yearning whenever he perceives any sincere spiritual grief. He notices and welcomes the slightest indication of repentance. "The eye of the Lord is upon them that fear him, upon them that hope in his mercy" (Ps. 33 : 18). The Heavenly Father sees the prodigal when he is "yet a great way off." He never "breaks the bruised reed," nor "quenches the smoking flax." If there be in any human creature the broken and contrite heart, the Divine Pity immediately speaks the word of forgiveness and absolution. The humble confession of unworthiness operates almost magically upon the Eternal. Incarnate Mercy said to the heathen "woman of Canaan" who asked for only the dog's crumbs, "O woman, great is thy faith; be it unto thee even as thou wilt" (Matt. 15: 28). The Omnipotent is overcome, whenever he sees lowly penitential sorrow. As "the foolishness of God is wiser than man," so the self-despairing helplessness of man is stronger than God. When Jacob says to the Infinite One, "I am not worthy of the least of all thy mercies," yet wrestles with him "until the breaking of the day," he becomes Israel, and "as a prince has power with God." (Gen. 32: 10, 24, 28). When Jehovah hears Ephraim "bemoaning himself," and saying, "Turn thou me, and I shall be turned," he answers, "Ephraim is my dear son. I will surely have mercy upon him" (Jer. 31: 18, 20).

Now the only obstruction, and it is a *fatal* one, to the exercise of this natural and spontaneous mercy of God, is the sinner's hardness of heart. The existing necessity for hell-punishment is not chargeable upon God. It is the proud and obstinate man who makes hell. It is his impenitence that feeds its perpetual fires. For so long as the transgressor does not grieve for sin, and does not even acknowledge it, it *cannot* be pardoned. Almightiness itself cannot forgive impenitence, any more than it can make a square circle.*

* Impenitence after sinning is a more determined form of sin, than sinning is in and of itself. For it is a tacit defence and justification of sin. If after transgression the person acknowledges

This is what gives to human existence here upon earth its dark outlook. Men are impenitent. They pay no heed to the voice of conscience; know little of remorse, nothing of genuine sorrow. They are stolid and lethargic in sin; or else angrily deny the fact. They bend no knee in self-abasement before the All-Holy; they do not cry, "O Lamb of God that takest away the sins of the world, grant me thy peace." Human life is gloomy and despairing, not because there is no mercy in the sweet heavens, but because there is no relenting, no softening, in the human heart. One is weary of hearing the incessant wail of the agnostic, and the cynic, over the "mystery" of this existence; the monotonous moan of the pessimist, that life is not worth living. One sincere confession of what the immediate consciousness of every man will tell him is the absolute truth respecting his character and conduct, when tried by a spiritual and perfect standard, would drive away this false

that he has transgressed, and asks forgiveness for so doing, he evinces that he does not excuse his act, or defend it. On the contrary, he renounces his act, condemns it, and mourns over it. But if after trangression the person makes no acknowledgment, and asks no forgiveness, he is really repeating and intensifying his sin. He virtually justifies himself in his act of rebellion against authority, and thus aggravates the original fault. It is for this reason, that impenitence for sin is more dreadful than sin itself. A penitent sinner can be forgiven; but an impenitent sinner cannot be. The former God pities, and extends the offer of mercy to him. To the latter God holds out no hope, because he cannot.

view of earthly existence as the miasmatic fog is blown by the winds. But instead of confessing sin, and imploring its forgiveness, men stand complaining of its punishment, or employing their ingenuity in endeavoring to prove that there is none; and then wonder that the heavens are black and thunderous over their heads. Not by this method, will the sky be made clear and sunny. Whoever will cast himself upon the Divine Compassion will find life to be worth living; but he who quarrels with the Divine Justice will discover that he had better not have been born.

What the human race needs is—*to go to the Divine Confessional.* The utterance of the Prodigal should be that of every man: "Father, I have sinned." The utterance of the Psalmist should be that of every man: "O thou that hearest prayer, unto thee shall all flesh come. Iniquities prevail against me: as for our transgressions, thou shalt purge them away." So long as man glosses over, or conceals, the cardinal fact in his history, he must live under a cloud, and look with anxiety and fear into the deep darkness beyond. It is useless to contend with the stubborn fact of moral evil by the ostrich-method of ignoring, and denying. The sin is here, in self-consciousness, terrible and real, the lancinating sting of pain and the deadly sting of death, in this generation and in all generations. Kant, the ethical and the metaphysical, is right when he affirms that the noumenon of sin is the dark ground under the phenomenon of life. *Confession*, therefore, is the only way to light and mental peace. The suppression of any fundamental form of human consciousness necessarily results in unrest. Man's words about himself must agree with his true character and condition; otherwise he becomes insincere, miserable, and false. The denial of moral evil is the secret of the discontent and melancholy with which so much of modern letters is filled. Rousseau made a confession, but not truthful, not humble; and hence it brought him no repose. Augustine made a confession, genuine, simple, thoroughly accordant with the facts of human nature; and the outpouring of his confidences into the ear of Eternal Purity and Mercy brought the peace that passes all understanding, and the immortal life that knows no melancholy, and no dissatisfaction. These historic persons are types of the two classes into which all men fall—the penitent and the impenitent.

The king in Shakespeare's Hamlet, writhing with selfish remorse but destitute of unselfish sorrow, in his soliloquy exclaims:

> "Try what repentance can: what can it not?
> Yet what can it, when one *cannot* repent?
> O wretched state! O bosom black as death!
> O limèd soul; that struggling to be free
> Art more engaged!"

Bunyan's man of Despair, in the iron cage, when assured by Christian that "the Son of the Blessed is very pitiful," replies: "I have so hardened my heart, that I *cannot* repent."

In these powerful delineations, these profound psychologists of sin bring to view a peril that environs free will. Pardon may be proffered by God, but *penitence may become impossible through the action of man.* "There are some sins," says Augustine, "that follow of necessity, from foregoing sins that occurred without necessity." The adoption of atheism is a sin without necessity. It is the voluntary action of man. But the hardness of heart that results from it, results of necessity. No man is forced to be an infidel; but if he is one, he *must* be an impenitent man. A luxurious and sceptical age should remember this. That man *cannot* repent, who drowns himself in pleasure, and never seriously reflects upon his accountability to his Maker. That man *cannot* repent, who expends the energy of his mind in the endeavor to prove that all human action is irresponsible, and the threatenings of Revelation an idle tale. They who have "eyes full of adultery *cannot* cease from sin" (2 Pet. 2 : 14). Absorption in worldliness, and adoption of infidel opinions, make repentance an impossibility. Sensuality and atheism harden the human heart, and render it impervious to the Christian Religion.

APPENDIX.

Note 1, p. 3. "The design of chastisement as such rests entirely in the person chastised; but punishment properly so called—for it may, of course, include sometimes an element of chastisement [as in human punishment]—has to vindicate the universal against the individual. Chastisement, accordingly, as that other word for it, discipline, implies (*παιδεία*, from *παῖς*), presupposes a tutorial relationship of which punishment as such knows nothing" (Müller, On Sin, I., 245, Urwick's Trans.).

Note 2, p. 6. Satan, in Milton's Paradise Lost (II., 274–278), suggests that custom may mitigate the pains of hell.

> "Our torments also may, in length of time,
> Become our elements; these piercing fires
> As soft as now severe; our temper changed
> Into their temper; which must needs remove
> The sensible of pain."

Note 3, p. 7. Respecting this very common objection, that the misery of a part of the human race will interfere with the happiness of the remainder, Müller (On Sin, I., 239) makes the following remark: "The primary meaning of *κρίσις* is discrimination and separation, and implies that the main contrast between man and man in relation to the future state is made manifest by the *cessation of intercourse* between those who obey God, and those who resist him. Beings whose relations to God are diametrically opposite, and persistently so, differ so greatly from each other that other ties of relationship become as nothing in comparison. Bonds of union among men arising out of the relationships of natural life must give way of themselves, if the tie which binds man's spiritual consciousness and will to his Creator be on either side wholly severed. For those bonds have not in themselves an eternal significance, save so far as they are included in that relation to God which is of everlasting importance."

Note 4, p. 22. The mythological explanation of Sheol, or Hades, prevails considerably at present. Many evangelical exegetes assert that the Biblical Hades is an under-world for all souls, and not a place of retribution. They support their opinion principally by the Rabbinical writings, the Greek and Roman classics, and the records of Egypt, Assyria, and Babylon. This assumes that there is no essential difference between the Hades of Scripture and that of the nations; that the inspired mind took the same general view with the uninspired, of the state of souls after death; that Moses, Samuel, David, and Isaiah, together with Christ and his Apostles, agreed in their eschatology with Homer, Plato, Virgil, the Egyptian "Ritual of the Dead," and the Babylonian tablets. A close adherence to the text and context of Scripture shows, we think, that this assumption is unfounded.

Increasing knowledge of the national religions has surrounded the Scriptures with a great mass of illustrative material which demands good judgment in its use. The tendency, of late, has been to forget that Divine Revelation is complete in itself and self-interpreting, and therefore must, first of all, be examined in its own light. Christianity may be illustrated by ethnical religion when the latter coincides with the former, not when it conflicts with it. When mythology is an echo, even broken and imperfect, of Revelation, it may be employed to explain it, but not when it contradicts. Scripture must rectify mythology, not mythology scripture. The meaning of Sheol, or Hades, should be obtained by comparing scripture with scripture, not by conforming scripture to the workings of man's imagination as he peers into the darkness beyond the grave, and endeavors to *image* to himself the abode of departed spirits. The mythological eschatology is a fanciful and picturesque conjecture respecting the unseen world. The Biblical eschatology is the sober unimaginative account of it by an eye-witness—namely, God speaking through prophets, apostles, and his Son Jesus Christ, who "came forth from the Father into the world, and, again, left the world, and went to the Father" (John 16 : 28).

Note 5, p. 23. Additional texts which prove that Sheol is a retributive evil denounced against sin and sinners are: Prov. 7: 27, "Her house is the way to sheol, going down to the chambers of death." Ps. 86 : 13, "Great is thy mercy toward me: and thou hast delivered my soul from the lowest sheol." To explain this latter passage as meaning only that God had raised the writer from a bed of sickness, or delivered him from some earthly calamity, disagrees with the entire Psalm—which is a prayer for spiritual and eternal blessings, and a thanksgiving for them. "Thou, Lord, art good, and ready to *forgive*, and plenteous in *mercy* unto all that call upon thee" (ver. 5).

Note 6, p. 28. Additional Old Testament texts teaching a future judgment are: Deut. 7 : 10, "The Lord thy God repayeth them that hate him to their face, to destroy them: he will not be slack to him that hateth him, he will repay him to his face." Job 21 : 19, 20, 30, "God layeth up his iniquity: he rewardeth him, and he shall know it. His eyes shall see his destruction, and he shall drink of the wrath of the Almighty. The wicked is reserved to the day of destruction: they shall be brought forth to the day of wrath." Ezek. 22 : 21, 22, "I will gather you, and blow upon you in the fire of my wrath, and ye shall be melted in the midst thereof. As silver is melted in the midst of the furnace, so shall ye be melted in the midst thereof: and ye shall know that I the Lord have poured out my fury upon you." Prov. 16 : 14, "The Lord hath made all things for himself: yea, even the wicked for the day of evil."

For a full citation of the Old Testament passages that teach the final judgment, see Edwards, On God's Moral Government. Works, I., 574–582.

Note 7, p. 35. That "the heart of the earth" means the grave, Witsius (Apostles' Creed, Dissertation XVII.) argues in the following manner: "Jonah says, that while he was in the bowels of the fish, he was 'in the belly of hell,' or of the grave, and 'in the midst (Heb., heart) of the sea;' and in this respect he was a figure of Christ placed in the heart of the earth. This does not mean the hell of the damned which, as Jerome says, is commonly said to be 'in the midst of the earth;' but an earthen receptacle, which has earth above, below, and on every side—or more briefly, which is within the earth. As the Scripture places Tyre 'in the heart of the sea,' that is, surrounded by the sea; as 'the way of a ship is in the heart of the sea,' when it is surrounded on all sides by the sea; as Absalom was 'alive in the heart of the oak,' that is, in the oak, within its branches—so the grave is 'the heart of the earth.' Chrysostom remarks that 'the sacred writer doth not say in the earth, but in the heart of the earth, that the expression might clearly denote the grave, and that no one might suspect a mere appearance [of death].'"

Note 8, p. 36. This text and Gen. 42 : 38, are parallel to Gen. 37 : 35, and explain Jacob's words, "I will go down into sheol, unto my son." "Gray hairs" cannot descend to an under-world.

Note 9, p. 36. That Sheol in Job 17 : 13 means the grave, is proved by the rest of the passage: "I have made my bed in the darkness. I have said to corruption, Thou art my father; to the worm, Thou art my mother, and my sister." Another conclusive text is Ps. 141 : 7, "Our bones are scattered at the mouth of sheol."

Note 10, p. 40. To the objection that Jacob knew, or supposed, that his son had been devoured by wild beasts, and consequently had no grave, and, therefore, meant to say that he should go down to the world of spirits to meet him, Rivetus (Exercitatio CLI. in Gen.) replies as follows: "Per *sepulchrum* non intelligimus strictè, id de quo apud jurisconsultos disputatur, cum agunt de sepulchro violato, sed id referimus ad rationem humationis in genere, quandocumque modo terra reddatur terrae, juxta sententiam divinam, 'Pulvis es, et in pulverem reverteris.' Sepeliri enim dicuntur quicunque terrae redduntur, etiam qui sepeliuntur 'sepulturaasini,' quod de Joachimo pronuntiavit Jeremias, Cap. 22, vers. 19. Igitur verba Jacobi 'Descendam ad filium meum lugens in infernum,' id est, in sepulchrum, non possumus melius explicare quam verbis Albini, qui sic ingemiscentis patris exponit querelam: 'In luctu permanebo, donec me terra suscipiat, ut filium meum sepulchrum jam suscepit.' Id ipse Jacob etiam intellexit, qui per vocem Sheol locum denotat 'quo senum *cani* cum dolore deducuntur.'"

Note 11, p. 42. Theodoret remarks on the words, "Hell from beneath is moved for thee, to meet thee," etc., that "it is the custom of Scripture sometimes to employ a figure, in order to state a thing more clearly. In this place the prophet introduces death as endowed with mind and reason, and expostulating with the king of Babylon" (Migne's, Ed. II., 334).

Note 12, p. 44. Müller regards it as so unquestionable, from the description in the parable of Dives and Lazarus, that Hades is not a place for repentance and salvation, that he places future redemption after the day of judgment. He asserts that "those theories of ἀποκατάστασις which represent it as taking place in the interval between death and the general resurrection directly violate the New Testament eschatology. If, therefore, the idea of an ἀποκατάστασις πάντων is to be maintained, it must be referred to a period lying beyond the general resurrection" (Sin, II., 426).

Note 13, p. 46. If Hades, in Rev. 20:14, means the under world, it includes Paradise, and Paradise is cast into the lake of fire. That Hades, in Rev. 6 : 8, is put for its inhabitants, is asserted by Eichhorn and Ebrard. Hengstenberg understands it to denote the place of torment (Speaker's Commentary on Rev. 6 : 8).

Note 14, p. 49. Additional Old Testament texts which teach the separation of the soul from the body at death, and the continued existence of the soul after the separation, are Gen. 49 : 33, "When Jacob had made an end of commanding his sons, he gathered up his feet into the bed and yielded up the ghost, and was gathered unto his fathers." Job 10 : 18, "Oh, that I had given up the ghost, and no eye had seen me!" Job 11 : 20, "Their hope shall be as the giving up of the ghost." Job 14 : 10, "Man giveth up the ghost, and where is he?" Jer. 15 : 9, "She hath given up the ghost." 2 Sam. 12 : 23, "Can I bring him back again? I shall go to him, but he shall not return to me." 1 Kings 17 : 21, 22, "And Elijah cried unto the Lord, and said, O Lord, my God, I pray thee let this child's soul come into him again. And the Lord heard the voice of Elijah; and the soul of the child came into him again, and he revived." Eccl. 8 : 8, "There is no man that hath power over the spirit to retain the spirit; neither hath he power in the day of death."

Note 15, p. 53. Additional texts which have no consistency, on the supposition that the Old Testament writers had little or no knowledge of a future blessed life for the godly, are the following: Gen. 17 : 7, "I will establish my covenant between me and thee, and thy seed after thee, in their generations, for an everlasting covenant, to be a God unto thee, and to thy seed after thee." Gen. 49 : 18, "I have waited for thy salvation, O Lord." Ex. 6 : 7, "I will take you to me for a people, and I will be to you a God." Deut. 33 : 3, 29, "Yea, he loved the people; all his saints are in thy hand. Happy art thou, O Israel: who is like unto thee, O people saved by the Lord." Job 13 : 15, "Though he slay me, yet will I trust in him." Isa. 33 : 22, "For the Lord is our judge, the Lord is our lawgiver, the Lord is our king; he will save us." Hab. 1:12, "Art thou not from everlasting, O Lord my God, mine Holy One? we shall not die." Ps. 31: 5, "Into thine hand I commit my spirit; thou hast redeemed me, O Lord God of truth."

It is impossible to confine this "covenant" of God, this "love" of God, this "salvation" of God, this "trust" in God, and this "redemption" of God, to this short life of threescore years and ten. Such a limitation empties them of their meaning, and makes them worthless. The words of St. Paul apply in this case: "If in *this* life only we have hope in Christ, we are of all men most miserable" (1 Cor. 15:19). Calvin (Inst., II., x., 8) remarks that "these expressions, according to the common explanation of the prophets, comprehend life, and salvation, and consummate felicity. For it is not without reason that David frequently pronounces how 'blessed is the nation whose God is the Lord, and the people whom he hath chosen for his own inheritance;' and that, not on account of any *earthly* felicity, but because he delivers from death, perpetually preserves, and attends with everlasting mercy, those whom he hath taken for his people." In the same reference, Augustine (Confessions, VI., xi., 19) says: "Never would such and so great things be wrought for us by God, if with the death of the body the life of the soul came to an end." When God said to Abraham, "Thou shalt go to thy fathers in peace" (Gen. 15:15), he meant spiritual and everlasting peace. It was infinitely more than a promise of an easy and quiet physical death. When Jacob, on his death-bed, says: "I have waited for thy salvation, O Lord" (Gen. 49:18), he was not thinking of deliverance from physical and temporal evil. What does a man care for this in his dying hour?

Note 16, p. 57. In proof of the unsettled state of opinion among the Fathers, on many points of doctrine, see Jeremy Taylor's Liberty of Prophecying, Section VIII.

Note 17, p. 58. Neander (II., 729, 730) shows that the later-patristic view respecting the state of unbaptized children was an important factor in the development of the mythological theory of the intermediate state. "The doctrine of the damnation of unbaptized infants, which, ever since the time of Cyprian, by the habit of confounding the inward grace with its outward sign, had become predominant, appeared to the Pelagians as something revolting. Yet even *they* made no distinction of the baptism of the spirit from the baptism with water. Accordingly, they must of necessity affirm, with regard to unbaptized infants, that, although exempt from punishment, they were still excluded from that higher state of being, and attained only to a certain intermediate state. And to the same result on this subject must everyone have been led, who was inclined to adopt the Oriental mode of considering the effects of baptism, and would consistently follow out the matter to a definite conclusion—unless he supposed a universal redemption or restoration as the final end, to which that intermediate state was destined to prove a point of transition for unbaptized infants. Such an intermediate state Gregory Nazianzen assigned for those who were unbaptized through no fault of their own. Augustine himself (De. Lib. Arbit., III., 23) had once entertained a like opinion." Neander adds that subsequently Augustine contended that "the notion of an *intermediate* place between the state of woe and the kingdom of heaven was a thing altogether unscriptural and incredible in itself; for man, being in the image of God, was destined to find his bliss in communion with God, and out of that communion could be no otherwise than wretched (De peccat. et rem., I., 58; Sermo, 294, 3). The Council of Carthage, A.D. 418, finally condemned, in its 2d canon, the doctrine concerning such an intermediate state for unbaptized children, on the ground that nothing could be conceived as existing between the kingdom of God and perdition, and affirmed the eternal perdition of all unbaptized infants."

Note 18, p. 58. The Heidelberg Catechism (Qu. 44), as did Calvin (Inst., II., xvii., 8–12), explains Christ's "descent to hell" figuratively, as denoting his piacular agony in the garden and on the cross. Witsius does the same in an exceedingly lucid and logical manner (Apostles' Creed, Dissertation XVIII.)

Note 19, p. 60. Dr. Charles Hodge (Theology, III., 716-756) presents and defends the reformed view of Hades in distinction from the patristic and papal, yet with some vacillation. On p. 734 he remarks that "there is no great difference between the [Rabbinical] Jewish doctrine of Sheol, in its essential features, and the true doctrine as presented by our Lord in the parable of the rich man and Lazarus. Both are represented as going into Sheol, or Hades." But on p. 736 he strongly combats that explanation, by "many modern interpreters," of St. Peter's discourse on the day of Pentecost, which makes him "to teach that the souls of the pious dead do not ascend to heaven, but descend to the gloomy abode of Sheol, Hades, or Hell—all these terms being equivalent."

Note 20, p. 61. The Pagan nomenclature is self-consistent, but the Pagan-Christian is not. In the Pagan scheme, Hades is a general term, having two special terms under it: namely, Elysium and Tartarus. But in the paganized Christian scheme, Hades does double duty, being both a general and a special term. When the Pagan is asked: "Of what does Hades consist?" he answers, "Of Elysium and Tartarus." But when the mythological Christian is asked: "Of what does Hades consist?" he answers, "Of Paradise and Hades." He cannot answer, "Of Paradise and Tartarus," because the latter is Gehenna, which he denies to be in Hades. Hence he converts the whole into a part of itself. To say that Hades is made up of Paradise and Hades, is like saying that New York City is made up of the Central Park and New York City.

Note 21, p. 62. The strong tendency of the later Jews to adopt both the customs and opinions of the heathen nations is noticed by Chemnitz in his learned and thorough examination of the Tridentine doctrine of Purgatory (Examen: De Purgatorio, Cap. II.) "Ex philosophorum ratiocinationibus, et ex superstitiosis gentium sacrificiis, quae ubique usitata erant, cum quidem sicut de caris absentibus ita etiam de mortuis naturalis quaedam cura et sollicitudo animis nostris insita est, ad Judaeos etiam hujus opinionis contagium quoddam, inclinato jam Judaismo, serpere coepit. Quanquam enim incisio carnis, et evulsio capillorum, in luctu mortuorum, expresse prohibita erant (Lev. xix., Deut. xiv.), ex conversatione tamen inter gentes, Israelitis etiam prophetarum tempore illa usurpari coepta fuisse, ex Jeremiae, cap. xvi., non obscure colligitur. Sicut a gentibus etiam tibicines in funerum curatione mutuati sunt (Math. ix.), juxta versum poetae: 'cantatat moestis tibia funeribus.'

"Eadem ratione tandem post prophetarum tempora, etiam orationes et sacrificia pro mortuis, Judaei imitari coeperunt circa annum 170 ante natum Christum, cujus exemplum extat 2 Maccabaeorum xii. Id quod tum fieri coepit, cum collapsa doctrina, et rebus omnibus, cum in imperio tum in templo, perturbatissimis, Judaei una cum foederibus, etiam lingua, appellationibus, moribus, et ritibus, conformitatem cum gentibus quaererent et affectarent: sicut tota historia Maccabaeorum ostendit."

Note 22, p. 62. As an example of the degree to which the mythological view of the condition of the dead had worked itself into the Christian church in the first part of the third century, take the following fanciful description of Hades by Hippolytus, in a fragment of his Discourse against the Greeks: "Hades is a place in the created system, unformed, beneath the earth, in which the light does not shine, and where there is perpetual darkness. This locality has been appointed to be, as it were, a guard-house for souls, in which the angels are stationed as guards, distributing to each one's deeds the temporary punishments for different characters. In this locality there is a certain place set apart by itself, a lake of unquenchable fire, into which we suppose no one has ever yet been cast:

for it is prepared against the day determined by God, in which one sentence of righteous judgment shall be justly applied to all. The unrighteous shall be sentenced to this endless punishment; but the righteous shall obtain the incorruptible kingdom, who, indeed, are at present detained in Hades, but not in the same place with the unrighteous. For this locality there is one descent, at the gate whereof we believe an archangel is stationed with a host. And when those who are conducted by the angels appointed for the care of souls have passed through this gate, they do not proceed on one and the same way; but the righteous, being conducted in the light toward the right hand, are brought into a locality full of light. There, there is neither fierce heat nor cold, but the face of the [O. T.] fathers and the righteous is seen to be always smiling, as they wait for the rest and eternal revival in heaven, which succeed this location. And we call it by the name of Abraham's bosom. But the unrighteous are dragged toward the left hand by the angels who are ministers of punishment, and they go of their own accord no longer, but are dragged by force as prisoners. And the angels appointed over them send them along, threatening them with an eye of terror, forcing them down into the lower parts. And when they are brought there, those appointed to that service drag them to the confines of hell (γέεννα). And the unrighteous hear the agitation and feel the hot smoke. And when that vision is so near that they see the excessively red spectacle of the fire, they shudder in horror at the expectation of the future judgment. And, again, when they see the place of the [O. T.] fathers and the righteous, they are also tormented. For a deep and vast abyss is set there in the midst, so that neither can any of the righteous from sympathy think to pass it, nor any of the unrighteous dare to cross it. Thus far, on the subject of Hades, in which the souls of all are detained until the time which God has determined; and then he will accomplish a resurrection of all."

The Koran has also borrowed from the patristic Christianity this view of the intermediate state. Paradise and Hades are represented as coterminous in an under world. "The inhabitants of Paradise shall call out to the inhabitants of hell-fire, saying, Now we have found that which our Lord promised us to be true; have ye also found out that which your Lord promised you to be true? They shall answer, Yea." (Koran, Ch. VII.).

Note 23, p. 65. Irenaeus (Adv. Haer. I. xxvii., 3) mentions as one of Marcion's heresies, his teaching that "Cain, and those like him, and the Sodomites, and the Egyptians, and others like them, and, in fine, all the nations who walked in all sorts of abomination, were saved by the Lord on his descending into Hades." Another opinion of Marcion, which Irenaeus mentions as heretical, was, that "Abel, and Enoch, and Noah, and those other righteous men who sprang from the patriarch Abraham, with all the prophets, and those who were pleasing to God, did not partake in salvation. For since these men, he says, knew that their God was constantly tempting them, so now they suspected that he was tempting them, and did not run to Jesus, or believe his announcement; and for this reason he declared that their souls remained in Hades." Irenaeus agreed with Marcion in regard to the assumed fact of Christ's descent to Hades, but differed from him in regard to its purpose and effects.

Note 24, p. 66. The abode of the demons is denominated "the abyss," in Luke 8:31. But, in Eph. 2:2, Satan is called "the prince of the power of the *air*." Ellicott's (in loco) explanation is probable. "As οὐρανος is used in a limited and partial (Matt. 6:26), as well as an unlimited meaning, so ἀήρ, which is commonly confined to the region of the air or atmosphere, may be extended to all that supra-terrestrial but sub-celestial region (ὁ ὑπουράνιος τόπος, Chrysostom) which seems to be, if not the abode, yet the haunt of evil spirits." See the authorities in favor of this explanation mentioned by Ellicott.

Hodge (On Eph., 2:2) regards ἀήρ as synonymous with σκότος. "The word σκότος, *darkness*, is so often used just as ἀήρ is here employed, as to create a strong presumption that the latter was meant to convey the same meaning as the former. Thus, 'the power of darkness,' Luke 22 : 53 ; 'rulers of darkness,' Eph. 6 : 12 ; 'the kingdom of darkness,' Col. 1 : 13, are all scriptural expressions, and are all used to designate the kingdom of Satan. This signification of ἀήρ is not without the authority of usage. The word properly, especially in the earlier writers, means the lower, obscure, misty atmosphere, as opposed to αἰθήρ, the pure air. Hence it means obscurity, darkness, whatever hides from sight."

Note 25, p. 67. The Council of Ferrara-Florence (1438–9), composed of Greek and Latin bishops, which endeavored to unite the Latin and Greek churches, decided "that the souls of the saints are received immediately into heaven, and behold God himself as he is three and one" (Taylor, Liberty of Prophecying, Section VIII.).

Note 26, p. 70. If both clauses are retained, the explanation proposed by Whitby (On Acts, 2 : 26, 27) is consistent with Scripture. "The Scripture doth assure us that the soul of the holy Jesus, being separated from his body, went to Paradise (Luke 23 : 43), and from thence it must descend into the grave or sepulchre to be united to his body, that this might be revived ; and thus it may be truly said : 'He was dead and buried ; his soul descended afterwards into Hades (the grave) to be united to his body ; and his body being thus revived, he rose again the third day.'"

Note 27, p. 72. The American Episcopal Church does not regard the "descent into hell" as a necessary part of the Christian faith. In the order for Evening Prayer, it is said that "any churches may omit the words, 'He descended into hell,' or may, instead of them, use the words, 'He went into the place of departed spirits,' which are considered as words of the same meaning in the Creed."

Note 28, p. 73. Van Oosterzee's (Dogmatics, II., 559, 560) history of the clause, "He descended into hell," is as follows :

"As concerns the history of this article, we find the conviction expressed, even by the earliest of the fathers—Justin Martyr, Irenaeus, Tertullian, Clemens Alexandrinus, and others—that Jesus, after his burial, actually tarried in the world of spirits, and by some of them, also, that he there preached the gospel; while the romantic manner in which this mysterious subject is presented in the apocryphal Gospel of Nicodemus is well known. Gnosticism, especially, warmly espoused this idea; according to Marcion, this activity of the Lord was directed to delivering the victims of the Demiurge, and leading them upwards with himself. From the symbols of the semi-Arians this much-debated article appears to have passed over to those of the orthodox church, according to some, with a view to controvert Apollinarism. In the Expositio Symboli Aquileiensis of Rufinus, this formula is found, and especially through his influence it appears also to have passed over into other confessions of faith; although it is remarkable that in the Nicene Creed mention is made only of 'was buried;' in the Athanasian Creed, on the other hand, only of 'descended into hell.' It is manifest from this that both expressions were first employed by many interchangeably, though very soon greater stress was laid upon the latter, and its contents regarded as the indication of a special remedial activity of the Lord. As the doctrine of purgatory became more developed, the conceptions found wider acceptance, that the Lord had descended into the lower world, in order to deliver the souls of the Old Testament believers from their subterranean abode, the limbus patrum. Especially under the influence of Thomas Aquinas, was developed the doctrine of the Romish Church, that the whole Christ—as to his divine and human nature—voluntarily repaired thither, to assure to the above-mentioned saints the fruit of his death on the cross, and to raise them out of this prison-house to the full enjoyment of heavenly blessedness. According to Luther, on the other hand, who regards the Descensus as the first step on the path of the exaltation, the Lord, after his being made alive according to the spirit, and, immediately upon his return from the grave, descended, body and soul, into hell, there to celebrate his triumph over the devil and his powers (Col. 2 : 15), and to proclaim to them condemnation and judgment. The Reformed theologians either understood the expression in the sense of 'buried,' or explained it of the final anguish and dismay of the suffering Christ. This latter is the view of Calvin (Inst., II., xvi.), and of the Heidelberg Catechism (Ans. 44). Some divines, the Lutheran Aepinus, *e.g.*, even maintained that the reference is to the sufferings of hell, which Christ endured in his soul, while his body was lying in the grave. No wonder that the Formula Concordiae declared this article to be one 'qui neque sensibus, neque ratione nostra comprehendi queat, solo autem fide acceptandus sit;' which, however, did not prevent its being possible to say, on the other side, that 'there are almost as many dissertations concerning the Descensus as there are flies in the height of summer' (Witsius). Left by the supranaturalism of the past century entirely in a misty obscurity, it was wholly rejected by the Rationalists, as the fruit of an exploded popular notion, to which, according to Schleiermacher, nothing but a fact wholly unnoticed by the apostles (unbezeugte Thatsache) served as a basis. Only in our day has the tide turned, and theologians of different schools have begun to return with increased interest, yea, with manifest preference to this dogma ; and to bring it into direct connection not only with soteriology, but also with eschatology." After this historical account, Van Oosterzee proceeds to defend the doctrine of a local descent to Hades, founding upon Ps. 16 : 10 ; Acts 2 : 25–31 ; 13 : 33–37 ; Eph. 4 : 8–10 ; 1 Pet. 3 : 19–21 ; 4 : 6.

Note 29, p. 75. It is objected that the phrase, he "*went* and preached" (πορευθεὶς ἐκήρυξεν), in 1 Pet. 3 : 19, would not apply to a preaching that was instrumental and spiritual. But the same use is found in Eph. 2 : 17 ; Christ "*came* and preached (ἐλθὼν εὐαγγελίσατο) to you which were afar off." The reference is to Christ's preaching to the Gentile world by his apostles. Christ, in his own person, did not preach to them which were "afar off;" and he forbade his disciples to do so until the time appointed by the Father; Matt. 10:5; Acts 1:4. See, also, Eph. 4:20, 21; Acts 26:23; John 10:16, for instances in which Christ's preaching by others is called his preaching.

Note 30, p. 77. "The Hebrew phrase, תַּחְתִּיּוֹת אֶרֶץ, to which the apostles' τὰ κατώτερα μέρη τῆς γῆς answers, is used for the earth in opposition to heaven, in Isa. 44:23; probably for the grave in Ps. 63:9; as a poetical designation for the womb in Ps. 139:15; and for Hades, or the invisible world, in Ezek. 32:24. [The context, however, shows that in this place, also, as in Ps. 63:9, it means "the grave." The "multitudes" of Elam, like those of Asshur, are "slain," and go down "to their graves."] Perhaps the majority of commentators take this last to be the meaning of the passage before us. They suppose the reference is to the descensus ad inferos, or to Christ's 'descending into hell.' But, in the first place, this idea is entirely foreign to the meaning of the passage in the Psalm on which the apostle is commenting. In the second place, there as here, the only descent of which the context speaks is opposed to the ascending to heaven. 'He that ascended to heaven is he who first descended to earth.' In the third place, this is the opposition so often expressed in other places and in other forms of expression, as in John 3:13, 'No man hath ascended up to heaven, but he that came down from heaven, even the Son of Man, who is in heaven.' (Compare John 6:38; 8:14; 16:58.) The expression of the apostle, therefore, means, 'the lower parts, namely, the earth.' The genitive τῆς γῆς is the genitive of opposition." (Hodge, on Eph., 4:9, 10.) Ellicott, in loco, while not adopting it, says that this is the interpretation "of the majority of recent commentators," and of Chrysostom and Theodoret among the patristic.

Note 31, p. 79. The common phrase, "Here, and Hereafter," denotes that human existence divides into only two sections. When Faust sells his soul to Mephistopheles, both parties understand that there are only two worlds—the temporal and the eternal. The former covenants with the latter as follows:

> "I to thy service *here* agree to bind me,
> To run and never rest at call of thee;
> When over *yonder* thou shalt find me,
> Then thou shalt do as much for me."

The same tremendous truth, that after the temporal the endless follows, is taught in the "mighty line" of Marlowe, in which he describes the emotions of Faustus as "the clock strikes eleven."

> "Ah, Faustus,
> Now hast thou but one bare hour to live,
> And then thou must be damned perpetually!
> Stand still, you ever-moving spheres of heaven,
> That time may cease, and midnight never come;
> Fair Nature's eye, rise, rise again, and make
> Perpetual day; or let this hour be but
> A year, a month, a week, a natural day,
> That Faustus may repent and save his soul!
> O lente, lente currite, noctis equi!
> The stars move still, time runs, the clock will strike,
> The devil will come, and Faustus must be damned."

Note 32, p. 82. The phrases, "end of the ages" (τέλη τῶν αἰώνων), 1 Cor. 10 : 11; "fulness of the time," Gal. 4 : 4; "fulness of times," Eph. 1 : 10; "these last days" (ἐσχάτος τῶν ἡμερôν τούτων), Heb. 1 : 1, denote the time of the Messiah's first advent—that epoch in the temporal αἰών when the incarnation occurred (Hodge on Eph., 1 : 10).

Note 33, p. 96. In Heb. 9 : 27, κρίσις is anarthrous: "after death cometh judgment." The writer does not say that *the* judgment immediately succeeds the death of the body, but that *a* judgment does.

Note 34, p. 105. The strange position has recently been taken, that the rejection of Christ is the only sin that brings eternal death. "No one," says Dorner (Christian Doctrine,

IV., 167), "will be damned merely on account of the common sin and guilt. But every one is definitely brought to [guilty] personal decision only through the gospel." Says a writer in the Andover Review (Dec., 1885, p. 574): "No one can be lost without the knowledge of Christ."

This implies that man's sin against the moral law is not sufficient to condemn him to eternal death. He must sin against the gospel before he can be so condemned. Neither original sin nor actual transgression, neither evil inclination nor outward crime, both of which are sins against the law, expose a man to hell.

This is an entirely new position, not to be found in the past history of eschatology, and invented, apparently, to furnish a basis for the doctrine of a future offer of redemption. The objections to it are the following: 1. It contradicts the whole tenor of scripture. Christ teaches that he came to call actual and guilty sinners to repentance (Luke 5:32); that he came to seek and save that which was really and truly lost (Luke 19:10); that he did not come into the world to condemn the world (because it was already condemned), but to save the world (John 3:17, 18). St. Paul affirms that the whole world, prior to redemption, and irrespective of it, are guilty before God (Rom. 3:19). St. John asserts that the whole world, Gentile and Jewish, unevangelized and evangelized, lieth in wickedness (1 John 5:19). To quote all the passages in which the Bible teaches that men are exposed to eternal death on account of their transgression of the law of God, would be to quote a large part of the Bible. The rejection of the gospel adds a new sin, and a very aggravating one, to the already existing sin against the divine law (John 15:22), but it is not the primary and original ground of condemnation. Men are punished, first of all, because they have sinned and come short of the glory of God (Rom. 3:23).

2. Secondly, unless man has already sinned against the law, he cannot sin against the gospel. If he has not previously committed a damning sin, for which Christ has atoned, he cannot reject Christ's atonement any more than an innocent angel

can. The rejection of salvation is meaningless, if no damnation has been incurred. If there is no disease, there can be no cure, nor rejection of a cure.

3. Thirdly, if no human soul is in danger of perdition until it has rejected Christ, then, if Christ had never been offered to man, no man would be lost. For if he were not offered he could not be rejected. In this case, it would have been infinitely better for mankind had Christ never come into the world on an errand of salvation. Had he remained unincarnate, as he had been from eternity, no one could have refused belief in him, and, as unbelief is the only damning sin, no one could have been damned.

4. Fourthly, if "no man can be lost without the knowledge of Christ," then none of the past heathen world who died without this knowledge incurred perdition for the "deeds done in the body," and none of the existing heathen world who are destitute of this knowledge are liable to perdition from this cause. In this case, it is matter of rejoicing that the past generations of pagans never heard of the Redeemer, and it should be an earnest endeavor of the Church to prevent all of the present generation of pagans from hearing of him.

Dorner's theory, that "no one will be damned merely on account of the common sin and guilt," is full of inconsistency and self-contradiction. First, he holds that man is in a state of "sin and guilt," but it is a species of sin and guilt that does not deserve endless punishment, and is not in danger of it. Secondly, he holds that man needs "salvation" from such an unendangered state. Thirdly, he holds that God is bound in justice to provide "salvation" from such an unendangered state. "The gospel," he says (IV., 167), "repentance and forgiveness of sins, is to be preached to all nations. This cannot refer merely to nations as unities, but must refer also to every individual; for otherwise the universality of the gracious purpose would not be sincerely meant; and *if God refused what is indispensable to salvation to the individual, condemnation would be impossible.*" Fourthly, he holds that God exhibits mercy, when he does what he is obligated to do.

To all this self-stultifying soteriology, the principle enunciated by St. Paul (Rom. 11 : 6) is a conclusive reply : "If by grace, then it is no more of works: otherwise grace is no more grace. But if it be of works, then it is no more grace : otherwise work is no more work." If man's "common sin and guilt" is not damning, then it is no longer sin and guilt : otherwise sin and guilt are no more sin and guilt. If Christ's salvation is not from eternal death and hell, then it is no longer salvation : otherwise salvation is no longer salvation. And if God's mercy is justly due to man, then it is no longer mercy : otherwise mercy is no longer mercy.

Julius Müller, though holding (upon the ground of Matt. 12 : 32) "the glorious hope that in the world to come, in far distant æons, some who here harden their hearts against God's revelation, and can expect only a verdict of condemnation in the day of judgment, shall find forgiveness and salvation" (Sin, II., 429), denies and combats Dorner's position that sin against the gospel is the only damning sin (Sin, II., 400). For a very able argument in proof that both evil inclination and outward transgression are damning, see Sin, I., 198–214.

Note 35, p. 108. For a powerful description of heathen depravity, see that of Thucydides, written with a pen of iron and the point of a diamond. "The plague introduced other and worse forms of lawlessness at Athens. Men who had hitherto concealed their indulgence in pleasure now grew bolder. For seeing the sudden change—how the rich died in a moment, and those who had nothing immediately inherited their property—they reflected that life and riches were alike transitory, and resolved to enjoy themselves while they could, and think only of pleasure. Who would be willing to sacrifice himself to the law of honor, when he knew not whether he should ever live to be held in honor? The pleasure of the moment, and any sort of thing which conduced to it, took the place of honor and expediency. No fear of God or law of man delivered a criminal. Those who saw all perishing alike thought that the worship or neglect of the gods made no difference. For offences against human law no punishment was to be feared; no one would live long enough to be called to account. Already a far heavier sentence had been passed and was hanging over a man's head; before that fell why should he not take a little pleasure?" (Jowett's Thucydides, B. II., 53). "When troubles had once begun in the cities men carried the revolutionary spirit further and further, and determined to outdo the record of all who had preceded them, by the ingenuity of their enterprises and the atrocity of their revenges. The meaning of words had no longer the same relation to things, but was changed by them as they thought proper. Reckless daring was held to be loyal courage; prudent delay was the excuse of a coward; moderation was the disguise of unmanly weakness; to know everything was to do nothing. Frantic energy was the true quality of a man. He who succeeded in a plot was deemed knowing, but a still greater master in craft was he who detected one. In a word, he who could outstrip another in a bad action was applauded, and so was he who encouraged to evil one who had no idea of it" (Jowett's Thucydides, B. III., 82). For a similar description of man acting from selfishness, see the "Plebeïan's speech" in Machiavelli's History of Florence, B. III., ch. iii.

Note 36, p. 109. The following extract from Witsius (Apostles' Creed, Dissertation II.) exhibits the hopeful view which the elder Calvinism took of the possible extent to which God's decree of election reaches: "Doctrines may be said to be necessary, either to salvation, or to religion, or to the church. A doctrine, without the knowledge and belief of which God does not save persons who have come to years of moral consciousness, is necessary to salvation; a doctrine, without the profession and practice of which no one can be considered religious, is necessary to religion; and a doctrine, without which no one is admitted to the communion of the visible church, is necessary to the church. There may be articles without which persons ought not to be admitted to the fellowship of the church, that should not, for that reason, be regarded as absolutely essential either to religion or to salvation. Although we might not dare to pronounce a sentence of condemnation against a particular man, we ought not, in defiance of order and discretion, to receive him forthwith into the bosom of our church, whatever sentiments he might hold, and to whatever sect he might belong. And with respect to religion, what falls within the sphere of duty is manifest. But how far it may please a gracious God, or how far it may be possible for him in consistency with his perfections and character, to extend his forbearance to anyone, and *save his soul*, notwithstanding his errors and sins; or, in short, what are the lowest attainments without which no man is saved—who can tell? For this distinction in doctrines, I am indebted to the celebrated Hornbeck (Socinianismi Confutatio, Tom. I., p. 209).

Again, the *knowledge* of those doctrines which are necessary to salvation admits of various degrees. It is in different measures of clearness, abundance, and efficacy, that divine revelation, the means of grace, and the communications of the Spirit are enjoyed; and a corresponding diversity takes place in the degrees of knowledge which the saints attain. In some it is clear, distinct, steady, and accompanied with a very firm and decided assent; in others it is more confused, more implicit and latent, subject to occasional wavering, and attended with an assent that is yielded with difficulty. The command of God, indeed, lays an indispensable obligation upon all men to make every possible effort to attain a most clear, distinct, and assured knowledge of divine truth. It cannot, however, be questioned, that the Deity, in his unbounded goodness, receives many to the abodes of bliss whose knowledge even of the principal articles is very indistinct, and such as they are hardly capable of expressing in their own words. The smallest measure of the requisite knowledge appears to be this, namely, that when an article of faith is *explained*, the mind so far at least apprehends it, as to recognize and *embrace* it as true.

Furthermore, *times* must be distinguished. It admits of

no doubt that under the bright dispensation of the Gospel, a more extensive and explicit knowledge is necessary to salvation than was required under the Old Testament economy; for it is reasonable that both knowledge, and the necessity of knowledge, should increase in proportion to the measure of revelation afforded. Under the Old dispensation, nay, during the time of our Saviour's abode on the earth, *it was possible for a man to be a true believer, and in a state of grace, who was ignorant of the sufferings, the death, and the resurrection of Christ,* and who even presumed to object to the testimony of Christ himself respecting these momentous topics, as is clear from the instance of Peter (Matt. 16 : 21–23); or, who, though he believed in general in the Messiah, yet knew not that Jesus is the Christ, as appears from the history of Cornelius the centurion (Acts 10 : 2–4). No one, however, I suppose, would now acknowledge any person [in Christendom] as a true believer, who should discover ignorance of these truths respecting the Lord Jesus; and still less a person who should contradict them when represented to him. On this subject, the remark of Thomas Aquinas (Secunda Secundae, i. 7) deserves to be quoted: 'The articles of faith,' says he, 'have increased with the lapse of time, not indeed with respect to the faith itself, but with respect to explicit and express profession. The same things which are believed explicitly, and under a greater number of articles by the saints in latter days, were all believed implicitly, and under a smaller number by the fathers in ancient times.'"

Note 37, p. 112. "It is a very significant fact that the subject of the book of Ruth is a *heathen* woman; she is, indeed, the *third* heathen woman in the genealogy of David and Christ, being preceded by the Canaanitess Tamar (Gen. 38) and the Canaanitess Rahab. Ruth is the most noble of all—a consecrated blossom of paganism, turning with a longing desire to the light and salvation of Israel. The fact that these three females are brought forward and ingrafted on the chosen line or family, conveys a very expressive lesson to the Israelites, abases their national pride, and bears testimony (by being both a fulfilment and a type) to all that had been promised to Abraham respecting his seed, namely, that in him should '*all* families of the earth be blessed' (Gen. 12 : 3). Of those who are blessed in the seed of Abraham, Naomi represents the people of God who are to proceed from the ancient people of the covenant, and Ruth represents those proceeding from the heathen world" (Kurtz's Sacred History, § 66).

Note 38, p. 113. The Thirty-nine Articles agree with the Westminster Confession in asserting that no man, either in Christendom or heathendom, can be saved by his morality and virtue. "They also are to be had accursed that presume to say, that every man shall be saved by the law or sect which he professeth, so that he be diligent to frame his life according to the law, and the light of nature. For Holy Scripture doth set out unto us only the name of Jesus Christ, whereby men must be saved" (Article XVIII.).

Note 39, p. 117. Toplady, one of the highest Calvinists of the Church of England, remarks as follows, respecting the salvation of all infants dying in infancy: "The rubric of the Church of England declares that 'it is certain by God's word that children which are baptized, dying before they commit actual sin, are undoubtedly saved.' I believe firmly the same. Nay, I believe more. I am convinced that the souls of all departed infants whatever, whether baptized or unbaptized, are with God in glory. And I think my belief warranted by an authority which cannot err—Matt. 18 : 14" (Church of England Vindicated).

Note 40, p. 120. Many of the arguments constructed against the doctrine of endless punishment proceed upon the supposition that original sin, or man's evil inclination, is the work of God—that because man is born in sin (Ps. 51 : 5) he was created in sin. All the strength and plausibility of John Foster's celebrated letter lies in the assumption that the moral corruption and impotence of the sinner, whereby it is impossible for him to save himself from eternal death, is not self-originated and self-determined, but infused by his Maker. "If," says he, "the very nature of man, as *created* by the Sovereign Power, be in such desperate disorder that there is no possibility of conversion and salvation except in instances where that Power interposes with a special and redeeming efficacy, how can we conceive that the main proportion of the race, thus morally impotent (that is, really and absolutely impotent) will be eternally punished for the inevitable result of this moral impotence?" If this assumption of concreated depravity and impotence is correct, Foster's objection to eternal retribution is conclusive and fatal.

Note 41, p. 120. For a discriminating and thorough statement of the aim of punishment, and its distinction from chastisement, see Müller on Sin, I., 244–251.

Note 42, p. 130. The intrinsic endlessness of guilt is vividly enunciated by Carlyle. "From the purpose of crime to the act of crime there is an abyss; wonderful to think of. The finger lies on the pistol; but the man is not yet a murderer: nay, his whole nature staggering at such a consummation, is there not a confused pause rather—one last instant of possibility for him? Not yet a murderer; it is at the mercy of light trifles whether the most fixed idea may not yet become unfixed. One slight twitch of a muscle, the death-flash bursts; and he is *it*, and will for Eternity be it; and Earth has become a penal Tartarus for him; his horizon girdled now not with golden hope, but with red flames of remorse; voices from the depths of Nature sounding, Wo, wo on him! Of such stuff are we all made; on such powder-mines of bottomless guilt and criminality—'if God restrained not,' as is well said—does the purest of us walk? There are depths in man that go to the length of lowest Hell, as there are heights that reach highest Heaven—for are not both Heaven and Hell made out of him, made by him, everlasting miracle and mystery as he is?" (French Revolution, Book I., Chap.

iv.). That such a view as this could be adopted of the nature of man's sin and guilt, and yet the Christian doctrine of atonement and redemption be rejected, is one of the contradictions in the history of human opinion.

Note 43, p. 131. "Those who are sent to hell never will have paid the whole debt which they owe to God, nor, indeed, a part which bears any proportion to the whole. They never will have paid a part which bears so great a proportion to the whole as one mite to ten thousand talents. Justice, therefore, never can be actually satisfied in the sinner's damnation, but it is actually satisfied in Christ" (Edwards on the Eternity of Hell Torments). The suffering of man is only relatively infinite; that of the God-man is absolutely infinite. The first is the suffering of finite persons in an endless but not strictly infinite time. The last is the suffering of a strictly infinite person in finite time. The element of infinity in the first case is relative; in the second case is absolute.

Note 44, p. 135. "Wrath will be executed in the day of judgment without any *merciful* circumstances. The judgments which God executes upon ungodly men in this world are attended with many merciful circumstances. There is much patience and long-suffering, together with judgment; judgments are joined with continuance of opportunity to seek mercy. But in hell there will be no more exercises of divine patience." (Edwards, Sermon XII.)

Note 45, p. 146.

"O fearful thought! one act of sin
Within itself contains
The power of endless hate of God,
And everlasting pains."

Faber's Hymn on Predestination.

Note 46, p. 151. St. Paul, in 2 Cor. 7:11, describes the willingness of a true penitent to suffer the punishment justly due to his transgression. "For behold this very thing, that ye sorrowed after a godly sort, what carefulness [against sin] it wrought in you, yea, what clearing of yourselves [apology], yea, what *indignation* [at sin], yea, what fear [of sin], yea, what vehement desire [of deliverance from sin], yea, what zeal [in resistance], yea, what *revenge* [self-condemnation]." The "indignation" and "revenge" arise from the sense of the intrinsic ill-desert and damnableness of sin.

Though the primary reference of this description was to the sin of the incestuous member of the Corinthian church, yet it had also a secondary reference to the sin of the church itself (1 Cor. 5:1, 2). The several emotions mentioned by the apostle are elements in the godly sorrow which the individual Christian experiences when he contemplates his own sin. He feels moral indignation at his own wickedness, and acquiesces in the retribution which it deserves.

Note 47, p. 151. Müller (Sin, I., 246) exposes the error of supposing that punishment is remedial in its nature, and adapted to produce penitence and reformation, in the following terms: "The distinctive purpose of divine punishment cannot be the improvement of the person punished, because this is the object of *redemption.* If punishment were the means appropriate to this end, there would be no need for redemption; or rather, if this object is attained by redemption, of what use is the severity of punishment? Are we to suppose that when redemption proves ineffectual for the improvement of man, punishment must be resorted to, to attain the object? It would then follow that punishment is more effectual for man's regeneration than redemption. The conflict between the sphere of punishment and that of redemption becomes all the more perplexing when we recollect that the main feature of redemption is the doing away with punishment by the forgiveness of sins. If punishment be remedial, is it a kindness to free man from it before it has accomplished its work? And how is it possible that redemption, which is the removal of punishment, should renovate, if punishment itself does so also?

And yet the influence of punishment in preserving and reestablishing the power of moral goodness in the sufferer must not be wholly denied. Punishment, on the one hand, acts as a barrier against the desolating inroads of sin by reasserting the fixed ordainments of the law; and, on the other hand, it bears witness to the sinner of the crushing power wherewith evil recoils upon himself, and makes him tremble when he surrenders himself to it. In these two ways, it *prepares* man for the work of redemption. But in its own distinctive nature, it is not adopted or calculated to produce a true improvement, an inward renovation of the sinner. On the contrary, the two spheres, that of redemption, which alone can accomplish a true renewal, and that of punishment, mutually exclude one another. Whenever a living participation in the blessings of redemption begins, punishment, properly so called—*δίκη, ἐκδίκησις, τιμωρία*—ceases; but, so long as man continues to be the subject of God's righteous punishment, he is excluded from those blessings (John 3 : 36)."

Twesten (Dogmatik, Th. II., § 39) argues in the same manner. "Punishment is not a proper means of reformation; for true reformation can issue only from free self-determination. It is voluntary in its nature. But a self-determination that is brought about by the fear of pain would not be moral, and of the nature of virtue. Any reformation effected from a selfish motive is not genuine reformation. Furthermore, if true reformation could be produced by punishment, why should not the legal and punitive method of the Old Testament have been the only one? The old economy was full of threatenings and penalties, and of fearful examples of their actual execution. Why did God send his Son, and make a new covenant and economy of mercy? Of what use is redemption, or the *remission* of punishment, if punishment is in itself healing and remedial? The Scriptures never represent punishment as reformatory. The proper punishment of sin is death (Rom. 6 : 23). As temporal death, which is the extreme penalty in human legislation, is not intended to reform the criminal, and reinstate him in human society, but forever cuts him off from it, so eternal death, in the Biblical representation, is not intended to be a means of educating the sinner and fitting him for the kingdom of heaven, but forever banishes and excludes him from it."

Note 48, p. 152. The doctrine that sin is an infinite evil and involves infinite guilt, because of its objective reference to an infinite Being, is one of the commonplaces of theology. Those who deny it, forget that the principle upon which it rests is one of the commonplaces of jurisprudence. The principle is this, namely, that crime depends upon the object against whom it is committed, as well as upon the subject who commits it. The merely subjective reference of an act is not sufficient to determine whether it is a crime. The act may have been the voluntary act of a person, but unless it is also an offence against *another person,* or persons, it is no crime. To strike is a voluntary act; but to strike a post or stone is not a culpable act. Furthermore, not only crime, but *degrees* of crime depend upon the objective reference of a personal act. Estimated only by the subjective reference, there can be not only no culpability, but no difference in culpability. Killing a dog is no worse than killing a man, if merely the subject who kills, and not the object killed, is considered. Both alike are voluntary acts, and of one and the same person. If, therefore, the gravity of the act is to be measured solely by the nature of the person committing it, and not by that of the thing against whom it is committed, killing a dog is as heinous as killing a man.

Now this principle of jurisprudence is carried into theology by the theologian. The violation of the moral law is *sin* and *guilt* only when viewed objectively in reference to God primarily and man secondarily. Viewed merely and wholly in reference to the transgressor himself, it is not sin and guilt at all. It is sin only as committed against God and mankind. Again, it is only the objective reference that will yield *degrees* of sin. One and the same act may be simultaneously an offence against an individual, a family, a state, and God. Measured by the nature and qualities of the offender himself, it has no degrees. But measured by the nature and qualities of these moral objects against whom it is committed, it has degrees of turpitude. As the first three are only finite in worth and dignity, the culpability is only certain degrees of the finite. As the last is infinite in worth and dignity, the culpability is infinite also.

Note 49, p. 156. That the perdition of some men seems to be settled in this life, is taught by St. Paul in 1 Tim. 5 : 24. "Some men's sins are evident beforehand (πρόδηλοι), going before them to judgment."

Note 50, p. 157. Müller alludes to unsensual and intellectual sin in the following terms: "That which makes sin to be sin, and which is the evil of evil, is the *selfish isolation* of the man which it involves. There are cases—with some it is the rule of life—where a man keeps himself free from wild ungovernable passions, and only seldom is guilty of overt acts which conscience recognizes as sins; yet in his inmost heart 'the *I*, that gloomy despot,' rules supreme; he stands alone in the world, shut up within himself, and in a chaos of selfish endeavors, preferences, antipathies—without any true participation in the joys and sorrows of mankind—estranged from God. In such a state, the principle of sin, though shut up within, rules with no less real power than where its dominion is manifest in glaring wickedness and vice, and a wild disorder of the outward life" (Sin, I., 136). He also notices that mere intellectuality is no certain preservative against sensuality and vice. "A superficial observation of life has led to the conclusion that immorality decreases in proportion as the growth of the intellectual nature increases, and the 'children of this generation' pride themselves in no small degree upon the discovery that culture and not Christianity is the means of true freedom, and the panacea for all the disorders of the world. But a single unbiassed and penetrating glance at life will suffice to dissipate these illusions. We oftentimes find the deepest moral degradation and disorder in the very highest stages of culture, a frivolity of mind resolving all relations of life into rottenness, an utter insensibility to every impulse of holy love, and a cold, calculating, self-conscious egotism, which puts from it the call to sacrifice anyone of its own interests as something altogether absurd—the men with whom it comes in contact being regarded merely as ciphers, by whose help its own aggrandizement may be attained. Mental culture does not eradicate a single tendency of moral depravity ; it only veils and refines them all ; and so far from redeeming the man, if it be not sanctified by a higher principle, it really confirms within him the dominion of sin " (Sin, I., 306, 307).

Note 51, p. 159. "There is this certainty," says Hooker (Polity, V., xlix.), "that life and death divide between them the whole body of mankind. What portion either of the two hath, God himself knoweth ; for us he hath left no sufficient means to comprehend, and for that cause hath not given any leave to search in particular who are infallibly the heirs of the kingdom of God, and who are castaways. Howbeit, concerning the state of all men with whom we live, we may till the world's end always presume that as far as in us there is power to discern what others are, and as far as any duty of ours dependeth upon the notice of their condition in respect to God, the safest axioms for charity to rest itself upon are these : 'He which believeth, already is the child of God ; and he which believeth not as yet, may become the child of God.' It becometh not us, during life, altogether to condemn any man, seeing that for anything we know there is hope of every man's forgiveness, the possibility of whose repentance is not cut off by death. And therefore charity, which 'hopeth all things,' prayeth also for all men."